Process
Thinking

Waymond Rodgers, *Throughput Modeling: Financial Information Used by Decision Makers.* Greenwich, CT: JAI Press, 1997.

Process Thinking

SIX PATHWAYS TO

SUCCESSFUL DECISION MAKING

Waymond Rodgers, Ph.D., C.P.A.

University of California

Author of Throughput Modeling: Financial Information Used by Decision Makers

iUniverse, Inc.
New York Lincoln Shanghai

Process Thinking
SIX PATHWAYS TO SUCCESSFUL DECISION MAKING

iUniverse books may be ordered through booksellers or by contacting:

iUniverse
2021 Pine Lake Road, Suite 100
Lincoln, NE 68512
www.iuniverse.com
1-800-Authors (1-800-288-4677)

ISBN-13: 978-0-595-38950-6 (pbk)
ISBN-13: 978-0-595-83334-4 (ebk)
ISBN-10: 0-595-38950-3 (pbk)
ISBN-10: 0-595-83334-9 (ebk)

Printed in the United States of America

Contents

Preface vii

CHAPTER 1 Pathways to Success 1

CHAPTER 2 Four Major Concepts that Govern Our Lives 10

CHAPTER 3 Why Framing Matters 35

CHAPTER 4 Why Information May Not Be Enough 52

CHAPTER 5 Judgment and Decision Choice 58

CHAPTER 6 The Expedient Pathway 65

CHAPTER 7 The Ruling Guide Pathway 73

CHAPTER 8 The Analytical Pathway 79

CHAPTER 9 The Revisionist Pathway 85

CHAPTER 10 The Value-Driven Pathway 92

CHAPTER 11 The Global Perspective Pathway 99

CHAPTER 12 Toward Successful Decisions with Process Thinking 107

Glossary 115

References 119

Index 123

About the Author 125

Preface

This book provides four dominant key concepts arranged into six pathways that can help improve our decisions. I have spent over 20 years studying how to combine perception, information, and judgment to help improve our daily lives with better process thinking. I have discovered that there are six pathways to an informed decision. The decision maker chooses one of these pathways, depending on the circumstances. Further, four major concepts are primarily used in this process—namely, perception, information, judgment, and decision choice. Anyone can drastically improve his or her decisions by adopting what I call *process thinking*. This book provides the essential ingredients to help you make better decisions in unstable environments punctuated by time pressures, lack of expertise, and incomplete information.

Our spiritual condition and state of mind are reflected in the decisions we make. Before these decisions are made, we travel down a particular pathway. A wrong pathway en route to a decision can twist our inner spirit and state of mind into a quagmire of doubt, despair, and destruction. Decisions are oftentimes difficult to make primarily because of our misunderstanding of the decision-making process. In the past, I have found myself wondering why I arrived at a particular decision. For example, when I was a teenager, I purchased my first automobile without knowing how to evaluate the important aspects of it. I had no idea how to compare the features of one automobile with another in a formal way. My decision was basically an emotional one, perhaps influenced by talking with the salesperson. I could have done a better job in comparing one automobile with another if I had the knowledge of a decision-making process, thereby saving thousands of dollars in repairs and maintenance. Traveling down the correct pathway would have enabled me to increase my overall satisfaction and well-being in making this type of decision.

To be knowledgeable in any decision-making area is to understand the interrelationships among perception, information, judgment, and choice. The process thinking model in this book will address and aid your decision-making processes in a comprehensive way. Because people often spend most of their time eliciting information in attempts to find or design alternative courses of action, a model is useful in understanding how they summarize credible evidence about the current situation. Process thinking also captures important elements from, and relevant to, a variety of different situations. This can provide predictions about subjects in which tasks will exhibit processes associated with the best pathway to a better decision. Finally, my model explicitly recognizes relevant developments in modern cognitive science, computer science, and management techniques.

Last, I believe this book can open a new vista for us regarding our relations with family, friends, acquaintances, and fellow employees. Our spiritual and mental well-being can open and drive an expanded array of possibilities leading to better decisions. Applying the decision-making pathway that is more suitable in a given situation can undoubtedly yield better results to us beyond a reasonable expectation most of the time. That is, using the appropriate pathway can save time, money, and energy leading to a decision. This book will provide you with very straightforward techniques for problem solving.

CHAPTER 1

Pathways to Success

> Someone has well said, "Success is a journey
> not a destination." Happiness is to be found
> along the way not at the end of the road.
>
> —Robert R. Updegraff

Process thinking dominates the type of decisions we make on a daily basis. It is about different pathways we use in order to make a decision choice. The pathway selected can affect the type of decision we make.

Six dominant pathways govern how we make decisions and what type of decisions we make. Taking the wrong pathway may lead to disastrous outcomes, including losing friends, careers, lifestyle, and wealth. Quite the opposite can occur by using the correct pathway in that it can result in success as represented by happiness, wealth, and friendship. This book takes an innovative and beneficial position to help guide us to a more constructive view of life. Further, it explores the major barriers to sound decision making, explains why framing problems is necessary, and advises when to use information for decision-making purposes.

Our spiritual and mental well-being are often depressed by misused perceptions and an inadequate use of information along with our inability to analyze and decide. We are all involved with *process thinking* when we make decisions. Process thinking relates to the different pathways we use to arrive at a decision choice.

A correct use of a decision pathway can result in making better decisions as represented by wealth, happiness, friendship, and career choices. We may begin to make a decision with all good intentions; however, situation after situation of using the wrong pathway can infect our spiritual and mental states. Decision making is used countless times a day, from waking up in the morning and deciding whether to brush our teeth first or to take a shower first, to deciding what we are going to eat for lunch or dinner. Decision making can also be very complex in terms of selecting a particular career or partner for life.

Although we have gained access to more information through technology, we have not been provided with the necessary models to help us classify and categorize these information sources. Living in an information and communication-intensive environment requires decision-making approaches that can help us to arrive at better decisions. Previous decision-making approaches have repeated the pitfalls of "thinking" a certain way. However, no previous approach has shown how a few major concepts can provide the six most effective pathways to a successful, appropriate, and constructive decision.

This book shows that decision making can be made in six different ways. Each varies by how much weight one puts on his or her perception or available information. The pathway you select can immensely influence the outcome of your decision! Given time pressures, unstable (changing) environment, incomplete information, and your expertise in a particular situation, a particular pathway can improve on your fortunes immensely. Further, your decisions will affect your spending habits, people you are associated with, family interactions, employment and investment opportunities, and your general well-being. This book provides insightful examples that can help you discover which of the six pathways is the most appropriate for a given situation.

Imagine that you are on your way home after a long and difficult day at school. You are very tired, hungry, and, most of all, very sleepy. You believe you have to satisfy your hunger immediately or else you might collapse. Therefore, you decide to stop at an unfamiliar restaurant and notice that the meals listed on the menu are familiar to you. However, you do not know the quality of the meals. What should you do? Before selecting on a course of action, certain factors usually enter into your deliberations.

Factors such as biases, search patterns, available information, time pressures, environmental conditions, and your own expertise on a particular matter should be considered. Knowing how these factors may influence your process thinking will undoubtedly improve your decisions. Four major concepts help guide our decisions. They are *perception (P)*, *information (I)*, *judgment (J)*, and *decision choice (D)*. These four concepts combine in various ways to provide us with six different pathways to making a decision. Typically, one of the six pathways provides us with the most successful, appropriate, and constructive decision. The six different pathways or processes that people undergo before reaching a decision are listed following. (Note: These pathways will be discussed in more detail in Chapter 2.)

(1) **The Expedient Pathway**   P→D
(2) **The Ruling Guide Pathway**   P→J→D
(3) **The Analytical Pathway**   I→J→D
(4) **The Revisionist Pathway**   I→P→D
(5) **The Value-Driven Pathway**   P→I→J→D
(6) **The Global Perspective Pathway**   I→P→J→D

Typically, our education, training, and life experiences do not help us in formalizing the necessary steps in making a decision. Four major concepts influence how decisions are formulated. The combination of these concepts provides much insight on how decisions are made. Interestingly enough, this book advocates that there are six major pathways to a successful decision based on these four major concepts. In addition, the pathway you take can drastically affect your decision choice.

Because of the complexities inherent in analyzing information, however, it is helpful for our decision-making processes to be guided in selecting, processing, and weighting the appropriate information for analysis. In this regard, we introduce the process thinking model (Fig. 1.1) as a means to assist individuals in their selective processing when confronted with a sea of information. Process thinking provides structure and unique functions in the process of information gathering and processing before rendering a decision. Although this process thinking has structure, it also allows enough flexibility for an individual to adjust, eliminate, and/or improvise information in supporting future actions. This process thinking perspective emphasizes the six dominant ways to arrive at a decision choice, as represented by Figure 1.1.

In Figure 1.1, *(1) P→D* represents the expedient pathway, whereby a person with a certain level of expertise or knowledge makes a decision without the benefit of information. *(2) P→J→D* depicts the ruling guide pathway, which emphasizes a person's perceived understanding of rules regardless whether the present information may be contradictory. *(3) I→J→D* highlights the analytical pathway, which includes a systematic and programmatic approach in using information. *(4) I→P→D* reflects the revisionist pathway, which is highly dependent on changing information. *(5) P→I→J→D* underscores the value-driven pathway, which indicates how an individual's perception helps channel and select certain types of information. *(6) I→P→J→D* represents the global perspective pathway, which assumes that the available information influences an individual's perception.

Although, other pathways contribute to the overall decision choice, more emphasis is normally placed on a single pathway. Within these pathways various searches for information, biases, and strategies are used in rendering a decision. However, depending on which pathway dominates, a particular approach to process thinking may lead to different decision choices.

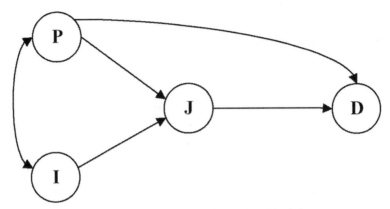

Figure 1.1. Process Thinking Model

Where P = perception, I = information, J = judgment, and D = decision choice.

We are constantly showered with a stream of information. Due to our bounded processing ability, only a limited amount of information is considered for further detailed analysis. Also, information may be noisy, inaccurate, complex, irrelevant, and/or misunderstood. In addition, our level of expertise can greatly influence the relevancy of information. Finally, time pressures and a changing environment can further introduce a high level of uncertainty to probable outcomes.

In our fast-moving economy, information and knowledge are becoming more and more dominant in decision-making tasks. Undoubtedly, this massive influx of information has been made possible by the coming of the "Information Age." Technology such as television, the Internet, and cellular telephones is constantly improving, thereby affecting and changing the medium by which we receive our information. For example, the Internet provides us with yet another way to communicate with our friends, relatives, neighbors, and fellow employees. The explosion of information has left us with the question, where do we begin and what types of information do we process before making a decision?

Well-known studies have documented the great difficulty that decision makers have with processing too much information. Given a sea of information, we as information processors have limited abilities to perceive, process, analyze, and make a decision.

People use coping skills to help size down the available information into a reasonable, much smaller, set to analyze for decision-making purposes. These coping skills oftentimes work marvelously well in basic or simple situations. For example, after I run out of the house with a cup of coffee in my hand, climb into my car, and pull away from the curb, I ponder a speech I have to give that morning while my street navigation is based primarily on a road map in my head. I am able to divert attention to my speech while relying on a set of memorized street coordinates to take me where I need to go.

Because analyzing information can be time consuming, complex, and difficult to understand, a useful model can assist us in arriving at a successful decision. In this regard, we introduce process thinking as a means to assist individuals in their selective processing when confronted with a sea of information.

Process thinking provides a unique and constructive way of formulating our thoughts into a successful strategy. This modeling process has structure while allowing for dexterity in the selection of an appropriate pathway. Process thinking depicts the interactions of four major concepts of decision making and problem solving. These four major concepts are perception, information, judgment, and decision choice.

Perception involves the process individuals use to frame their problem-solving set or view of the world. Framing explains how individuals see a problem based on their stored knowledge, which is implemented to solve a problem. That is, individuals react to situations as they interpret them, not as they exist in some objective world. Depending on the task at hand, this framing involves individuals' expertise in using preformatted knowledge to direct their search of incoming information necessary for problem solving or decision making.

Perception can be influenced by biases and strategies. Biases are a penchant for one particular point of view or perspective. A perspective relates to the content or reference from which to classify, categorize, measure, or codify experience forming a representational mental state.

Strategies are shortcuts or preprogrammed steps resulting in simplifying procedures, or rules of thumb, in making decisions. They are oftentimes automatic when we are processing information before taking any decision action. For example, if we are walking or driving to our place of employment, strategies can aid us arriving at our final destination point without recalling every street name or winding pathway. That is, we have automatized the procedures used in walking or driving from home to work.

Information includes the set of information available to a decision maker for problem-solving purposes. Generally, we hope that information is both reliable and relevant. *Reliable* relates to information sources as being correct, verifiable, or dependable. *Relevant* relates to information sources as being timely or sufficient to understand and implement in matters that are important to us. Typically, information is not complete, may have errors, or may be difficult to interpret.

The relevance and reliability of information can influence the particular pathway we use to make a decision. The reliability and relevance of information can be influenced by several factors. Identifying these factors will undoubtedly affect how you process it. Information used in decision making is influenced by uncertainty of occurrence (precise or imprecise), information type (precise or vague), and comparability of events or objects (precise or vague). Uncertainty of occurrence is *precise* when an exact probability can be calculated or proposed.

An example is calculating the probability that your new dishwasher will work properly for the next 365 days. A *vague* (imprecise) uncertainty is when, for example, you purchase a used vacuum cleaner and you do not know if it will operate correctly next year. Next, information sources are precise if they can be understood uniquely in one way. Information sources are imprecise or vague if they are not distinctly defined or cannot be understood in at least one precise way. Finally, events or objects are precise when they can be completely arranged or classified. For example, five apples are more than two apples. Events are vague (imprecise) when they cannot be completely arranged or classified, such as not being able to determine whether violets are more beautiful than roses and petunias.

The *judgment* function contains the process that individuals implement to analyze incoming information as well as influences from the perception function. From these sources, rules are implemented to weigh, sort, and classify knowledge and information for problem-solving or decision-making purposes.

Information is converted to knowledge once it is processed in the minds of individuals, and knowledge becomes information once it is articulated and presented in the form of text, graphics, words, or other symbolic forms. Therefore, knowledge can be viewed as the storage and organization of information in memory. Finally, *decision choice* represents an action either taken or not taken.

Summary

Every day we are bombarded by informational sources—some useful and some not—in our attempt to solve problems. A variety of problems exist in our daily lives from the simplest to the most complex. Typically, we address these problems without the benefit of tools directed at problem solving. As a result, we may solve similar problems on a daily basis in an inconsistent way. Or, to stay in our comfort zone, we may become overly conservative when confronted with a task to be solved.

Oftentimes, the process of decision making can deter, distract, or eliminate useful information in problem solving. Yet, there is not enough emphasis on pathways in decision-making models that can help us better understand the constant flow of information we receive each day.

Process thinking helps us to select the appropriate pathway for a successful decision. These pathways include (1) P→D, the expedient pathway, (2) P→J→D, ruling guide pathway, (3) I→J→D, the analytical pathway, (4) I→P→D, (5) P→I→J→D, the value-driven pathway, and (6) I→P→J→D, the global perspective pathway.

Why use *process thinking?* This modeling approach can alert you to the particular pathway you are using to arrive at a decision. The wrong pathway could lead to large dollar losses or a breakdown in relationships because of not understanding processing and informational biases. No matter how sophisticated the tools we use to analyze information, we are still hampered by strategies and biases.

Biases may also creep into our analysis before, during, and after we decide. In examining a vast amount of information, we sometimes use prior experiences or biases to select certain types of information for decision-making purposes. No matter how well attuned our thoughts or sentiments are, biased information can sometimes result in "garbage in, garbage out." Further, accounting for outcomes as opposed to decision making may increase your commitment to prior courses of action.

Reliance on outcomes heightens the need for self-justification, thereby increasing a desire to defend past decisions. However, the six pathways to success will (a) lead you to engage in more evenhanded evaluation of alternatives and (b) decrease the need for self-justification. Accordingly, the six pathways discussed in this book represent interesting ways we can act or influence others.

Taking the most appropriate pathway can lead to more efficient and effective decisions in our everyday life. Selecting the most appropriate pathway can lead to better financial, education, career, employment, and relationships decisions. The next chapter explores the intricacies of process thinking in greater detail.

CHAPTER 2

Four Major Concepts that Govern Our Lives

True wisdom is to know what is best worth
knowing, and to do what is best worth doing.

—Edward Porter Humphrey

This chapter provides a more detailed explanation of the four major concepts that govern our lives. These concepts are perception, information, judgment, and choice. In general, a successful journey along a pathway occurs when we are aware of the obstacles and shortcuts we will encounter. Not knowing what is included on a particular path is similar to not knowing what type of food you are eating. That is, is it poisonous or wholesome? A major feature in process thinking, discussed in chapter 1, is that it underscores which pathway works best, given a particular situation.

Your final decisions can change dramatically just by selecting the appropriate pathway for your process thinking. No one sets out to make a bad decision. However, as the old saying goes, "If you fail to plan, you plan to fail." Failing to recognize the four major concepts in decision making can contribute to poor planning. Not understanding our decision pathways can result in failure to keep an eye on things and in not taking action when our circumstances start to change. The rules, principles, or guidelines we don't follow often have a greater bearing on our decisions than those we do follow.

Perception—Defining the Issue

Perception refers to framing the decision-making process. To understand perception, you need to identify its classification and categorization dimensions. First, beginning within the perceptual function in the process thinking model in Figure 2.1, we define the problem. Individuals may make mistakes by (a) defining the problem in terms of a proposed solution, (b) missing the big problem, or (c) diagnosing the problem in terms of its symptoms.

For example, when you know society's views prior to forming your own perception, conformity may become the likely coping strategy. Individuals simply implement positions that are likely to gain the favor of those to whom they are accountable. This permits decision makers to avoid unnecessarily analyzing (judgment) the pros and cons of alternative courses of action, interpreting complex patterns of information, and making difficult trade-offs. These strategic shifts occur even if they produce inefficient decision outcomes.

Next, identifying the criteria or guidelines is influenced by the perceptual function as well. Most decisions require the decision maker to accomplish several objectives. Identifying all-important criteria in the decision-making process is essential to reduce perceptual biases.

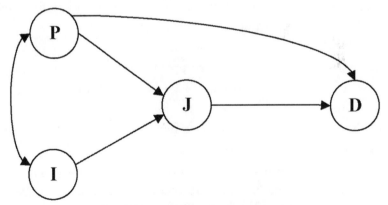

Figure 2.1. Process Thinking Model
Where P = perception, I = information, J = judgment, and D = decision choice.

Information Relevancy and Reliability

Information derives from all available stimulants to our five senses of tasting, seeing, touching, smelling, and hearing. Our senses provide us the means to collect information for later use in making decisions. Many of the inputs received from our senses are data. The data inputs can be viewed as unprocessed information. In other words, data becomes information when we judge it to be reliable and relevant.

Reliable relates to correctness, reproducibility, and dependability. Relevance has to do with relating information to past, present, and/or future events (timely). It provides us with the ability (understandability) to take action or not, depending on the circumstances.

Information can be divided into political, economic, management, financial, and social elements. *Political* information pertains to the legal organization of an entity as well as the reality of how the entity functions. *Economic* information relates to events outside the control of individuals or organizations. These events generally include changes in government policies, purchasing habits of customers, union contracts, emerging technologies, and so forth.

Management information refers to how people relate to each other. This includes, for example, supervisor–employee, parent–children, and individual-to-individual relationships. Information gathered about these types of relationships measures how people process information as well as how they implement their objectives and goals.

Financial information pertains to monetary matters. This type of information can be viewed as liquidity, profitability, and risk features of an individual or organization. Liquidity is associated with the ability to use cash to manage day-to-day needs. Profitability has to do with an individual's ability to generate income beyond expenses. Risk relates to individuals' or organizations' level of debt.

Social information deals with the cultural, ethical, and trust systems that shape our lives. For example, the enforcement of obligations, promises, and expectations occurs through social processes that encourage customs of flexibility, solidarity, and information exchange.

Without reliable and relevant information, however, it is difficult to confirm whether objectives in these areas have been achieved. Relevant and reliable information needs to be in place to determine whether the objectives have been met. We are interested in not only decomposing information into its most elemental components but also in treating it as a natural bridging mechanism between the decision maker and various levels of analysis. Information that governs our choices is complex as well as fluid and dynamic. As varying pieces of information interact, we put together subtle patterns of relationships to aid our understanding and analysis.

Judgment Function—Analysis of Perception and Information

Judgment refers to the sorting and ranking aspects of the decision-making process. To understand judgment, it is necessary to identify the components of the decision-making process that require analysis. First, given the perceptual framing of the situation, we identify the problem. Next, we identify and weight the criteria or guidelines. Then we generate alternatives of possible courses of action. We proceed to rate each alternative on each criterion before computing a decision.

In the process of making a judgment, we use two methods to analyze perception and information: compensatory and noncompensatory. In the compensatory method, when selecting between two choices, we determine the essential criteria needed to make a comparison. Next, we sum the weights of each of the items to determine which has the highest value.

For example, let's assume a comparison between DVD player one and DVD player two needs to be made for a purchase decision. Let's further assume we rate these products on the following three criteria: maintenance agreement, sound quality, and price. We check with a reputable independent third party to determine the values placed on these three criteria.

Based on a ten-point scale, with ten representing the highest positive values, player one has the following values: maintenance agreement (5), sound quality (9), and price (6). The total points equal 20 (5 + 9 + 6). Player two has the following values: maintenance agreement (9), sound quality (7), and price (8). The total points equal 24 (9 + 7 + 8) for player two. Therefore, our analysis indicates that player two (24 points) ranks higher than player one (20 points). Hence, if a purchase is to be made based on our analysis, then it should be player two. This method of analysis allows us to add and sum the product criteria values and make a decision based on the product with the highest value.

The noncompensatory strategy for analysis allows us to modify the basic compensatory strategy of adding and summing the criteria values. That is, an analysis of only one criteria value of the product may be necessary.

For example, selecting a meal with the best taste, regardless of other attributes such as price, restaurant location, servers' friendliness, or calorie count, results in these other criteria being ignored. Or a selection of a product or service may be based on certain ranges of values for each of the criteria. For example, turning back to the previous example on selection of DVD players, a noncompensatory strategy may include a ceiling price. That is, a price of more than $200 would eliminate any particular model from further consideration.

Decision Choice Representing a Course of Action

Finally, the solution with the highest expected value should be selected as our decision choice. This concept includes the selection of the best alternative solution or course of action. During process thinking steps, individuals implement their abilities to ensure that a decision follows their intended plans.

Dominant Decision-Making Pathways

The following sections briefly highlight the six dominant decision-making pathways. These pathways, when used appropriately for a given situation, can affect your success in investments, marriage, career opportunities, and general satisfaction. Each pathway will be covered in more detail in later chapters. These six pathways are described as follows.

1. The Expedient Pathway   P→D
2. The Ruling Guide Pathway   P→J→D
3. The Analytical Pathway   I→J→D
4. The Revisionist Pathway   I→P→D
5. The Value-Driven Pathway   P→I→J→D
6. The Global Perspective Pathway I→P→J→D

P→D: Where Your Perception Leads Directly to a Decision Choice

The Expedient Pathway (P→D) represents an individual with a certain level of expertise in making a decision without the aid of information because the information is too noisy, incomplete, or inadequately understood, or the alternatives cannot be differentiated. Also, time pressures may prevent an individual from analyzing the available information.

With respect to professionals or experience types, decision makers rely on their experience, training, and education (see Fig. 2.2). This pathway is proper when you cannot rely on available information or are faced with serious time pressures to make a decision. This pathway, when used correctly, can decrease inhibitions, anxieties, or procrastinations, thereby freeing you to engage into other pursuits.

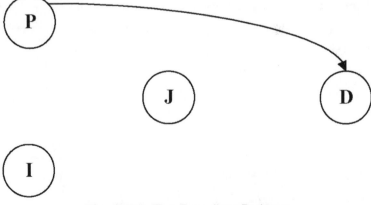

Figure 2.2. The Expedient Pathway
P→D: Process thinking is a decision made based on perception only.

Next, some examples illustrate successful use of the pathway, whereas others show how a particular pathway can lead to an erroneous or less-than-satisfactory result.

P→D Pathway Example 1: A group of people at a party has gathered to discuss world events. Imagine an individual in the group, who has a severe stuttering problem, beginning to lead a discussion on the complexities of global warming. The other group members might assume that this person does not understand the complexities surrounding global warming issues because he or she cannot articulate well. That is, they are making this decision based on perception (the person's stuttering) without consideration of any outside factors, such as the person's education or knowledge. Hence, the use of this particular pathway can lead to an erroneous conclusion about the person.

P→D Pathway Example 2: The eyes of deer, elk, and other wildlife shine (or reflect back) in vehicle headlights, permitting drivers to see their eyes in the darkness. Therefore, I have learned to look out for animals along the road at night. Consequently, when I am driving on a highway at night and suddenly a large deer races onto the road, I quickly swerve to avoid hitting the deer. I perceive that the deer is directly in front of me, and I know if I hit the deer, I will seriously hurt it. The *I* (information) function is minimized, in that there is not sufficient time to analyze more information about my surroundings or why the deer is in the road. Because immediate action is required, the *J* (judgment) function is not called on, but my perception is relied on to make a quick decision.

P→D Pathway Example 3: The chances of anyone being kidnapped or taken hostage are small. If it does happen, chances of survival are high. Kidnapping is a terrifying experience, but people normally possess more personal resources than they realize to cope with the situation. Whenever television stations or newspapers report about the kidnapping of a civil servant by a militant group, our immediate response is most likely anger toward the militant group responsible for the action.

The militant group is viewed as "terrible individuals." We do not typically seek information to determine whether the kidnapped person was a Samaritan or a murderer, nor do we take into consideration that some of the militants have joined the insurgency out of fear for their own lives. We simply denounce the militants for their actions (*decision choice*).

The P→D (Expedient Pathway) examples demonstrate that given a strong reliance on perception, the information and detailed analysis (judgment) functions may not be necessary when making a choice.

In addition, these examples highlight that information processing may be hampered as a result of time pressures, a rapidly changing environment, and/or information being incomplete, noisy, difficult to interpret, or unmanageable. In other words, the information function and the judgment function are neither relied on nor relevant to a decision task at hand. Therefore, the P→D pathway provides for the most efficient and direct path to a decision choice. Although this particular pathway may not result in the right decision, given the circumstances, it may be the best pathway to take to a decision.

P→J→D: Where Your Perception Leads to Judgment, Then to a Decision Choice

The Ruling Guide Pathway (P→J→D) generally relates to a *no*-time-pressure situation, and the individual is confronted with a changing or unstructured environment (e.g., attempting to predict where to vacation ten years from today). Also, incomplete and noisy information, inadequate understanding, and undifferentiated alternatives may contribute to an individual ignoring the present available information (Fig. 2.3). This pathway is guided by a person's internal or external rules or laws, regardless of whether the present information may be contradictory. If you adopt this pathway, the present information available to you is either downplayed or ignored. Depending on the situation, such a pathway can lead to either beneficial or unpleasant results.

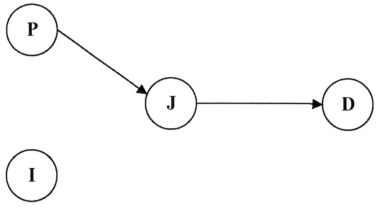

Figure 2.3. The Ruling Guide Pathway
P→J→D: Process thinking is based on Perception to Judgment to Decision.

P→J→D Pathway Example 1: Although comedy is subjective, certain aspects about a great stand-up act separate the amateurs from the professionals. These include how to deal with issues such as (but not limited to) political incorrectness, vulgarity, timelessness, and the uncontrollable urge to repeat another comedian's jokes.

A stand-up comedian is telling jokes regarding various controversial issues such as sexuality and religion, and she wants to tell jokes that make fun of Democrats. First, as a rule, she will use her perception to frame how the audience is receiving the other jokes and then make an analysis (judgment) regarding the audience sensitivity to political jokes. Because the comedian has no information on whether the audience majority is Democrats or Republicans, she must utilize her perceptual framing of the situation. This frame could be how the audience related to the previous jokes, whereas the analysis (*judgment*) is how they will react to making fun of Democrats. The joke will be told if the analysis supports this decision (*decision choice*).

$P\rightarrow J\rightarrow D$ Pathway Example 2: The foremost cause of fires in the United States is the daily act of cooking, when stoves and ovens often are left unattended. The most frequent cause of death from fire is careless smoking. Other widespread sources of house fires include unattended portable heaters, overloaded electrical circuits or extension cords, inadequately located electrical wires, unattended fires in fireplaces, gas grills, and malfunctioning clothes dryers.

I am situated in my upstairs bedroom when I suddenly realize that my house is on fire. The two options of escaping are (1) navigating my way through the house and escaping through the front door or (2) climbing out my bedroom window. If I attempt to run downstairs and through the house, I risk getting trapped or badly burned. If I choose to jump through my window, then I risk breaking my legs. I analyze my two options and decide to climb out my window. In this situation, I do not have sufficient information regarding which areas of the house are on fire, and I do not have the time to gather further information.

$P\rightarrow J\rightarrow D$ Pathway Example 3: Perception influencing judgment during to a decision occurs when information is either absent, flawed, or ignored. Typically a salesperson needs to give a potential customer a reason to buy his product or service at their door. Suppose you have been approached by a salesperson offering a fantastic promotion or an incredible discount that is only being promoted door-to-door. When confronted by the door-to-door salesperson (*perception*), many people ignore the information presented and only try to judge (*judgment*) the sincerity of the salesperson.

If salespeople are perceived to be dishonest, they could be turned away even though the product has a good brand name. On the other hand, if the salesperson is a child working on a school fund-raiser, then that child might make a sale even if the product is grossly overpriced. If the child is perceived (*perception*) to be nice and judged (*judgment*) to be innocent, then the decision to buy may be positive (*decision choice*). This ruling guide example may very well lead to a bad decision in that the purchase of an inferior product is not a function of the product, but is based, rather, on the characteristics of the salesperson.

The P→J→D (Ruling Guide Pathway) examples illustrate that the perception and judgment concepts are used exclusively, without the need for any reliable and relevant information. Therefore, a decision choice is made by the linkage of perception through *judgment* (analysis). Also, time pressures and the instability of the environment are not as extreme, compared with the P→D pathway (Expedient Pathway). However, information that is not utilized, as a result of its incompleteness, noisiness, interpretation difficulties, or alternatives, is unmanageable to order in a useful manner.

A prime characteristic of the P→J→D pathway is that it functions based on some type of rules or preamble. That is, once a particular procedure or method is studied, memorized, or practiced, it becomes a driving force in the *perception* process. This embedded procedure activates the analysis process (*judgment*) to follow a prescribed set of rules that are applied to a situation, which requires a decision. Last, the P→J→D pathway helps guide us by providing a road map that decision makers can follow to arrive at a decision.

I→J→D: Where Information Leads to Judgment, Then to a Decision Choice

The Analytical Pathway (I→J→D) represents an analytical and programmatic approach, which includes specifying the problem, identifying all factors, weighting factors, identifying all alternatives, rating alternatives on each factor, and choosing the optimal alternative (Fig. 2.4). The use of this pathway assumes that the information you are analyzing is reliable and relevant. In addition, you should assume that information representing important criteria or attributes of a person, place, or thing can be properly weighted in terms of importance. Of course, if the information you use is incomplete or the environment is changing, rendering the information not relevant, then the use of this pathway may lead you to bad decisions.

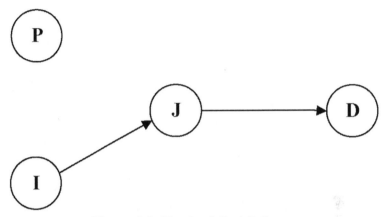

Figure 2.4. The Analytical Pathway
I→J→D: Process thinking goes from Information to Judgment, then to Decision.

I→J→D Pathway Example 1: When a purchaser has fallen behind on payments in a retail installment sale, a dealership has several options, including repossession. Unfortunately, dealerships or lenders usually have the right to repossess a vehicle after any late payment (including the very first one). It's beneficial to always read the fine print in your credit contract because it outlines the lender's right to repossess an automobile and what a person can be charged for the repossession. The loan contract must disclose the lender's repossession policy, including when they can repossess and what your rights are if repossession occurs.

Several states have specific repossession laws, and these laws are usually referenced in the credit contract. Assume that an automobile dealership is the lender and repossesses automobiles based on three consecutive missed payments by the customer (*information*). This guideline applies to everyone without exceptions. Despite the fact that the dealership owner knows about hardships confronting a customer, such as payment of mounting hospital bills, the dealership must rely only upon information received from the billing department that pertains to three consecutive missed payments. The dealership verifies this information by its analysis (*judgment*) and makes a decision (*decision choice*) to repossess the automobile.

I→*J*→*D* Pathway Example 2: Viruses cause colds; in fact, there are over one hundred different viruses that cause colds. There are no medicines to cure colds. Antibiotics are only useful against bacteria, not viruses. Nevertheless, a variety of products are available to assist in treating the symptoms of a cold. Many of these can be bought without a prescription. The main types of over-the-counter cold medicines are analgesics, antitussives, expectorants, and oral decongestants. Analgesics relieve aches and pains and reduce fever. Antitussive medications help you stop coughing. Expectorants help to clear phlegm, an abnormal product of mucus, from the lungs. Oral decongestants are drugs that help to reduce congestion.

Assume that you are not familiar with brand-name cold medicines. Therefore, when deciding which cold medicine to purchase, you use a compensatory method to sort through the information. The important attributes are how the medicine tastes, whether it causes drowsiness, time duration of the medicine effects, and price (*information*). You input the information for each attribute of the cold medicine product and then rank the products from high scores to low scores (*judgment*). After the ranking, you purchase the product with the highest score (*decision choice*).

I→*J*→*D* Pathway Example 3: You are considering taking a summer vacation. There are several options, all of which appear equally attractive to you. Therefore, you gather information on several dominant vacation attributes such as airfares, hotel prices, availability of tourist attractions, and ease of transportation. One of your decision rules is to eliminate all packages that do not conform to a two-week tour schedule, because of your vacation time. Vacation places are eliminated in which you are unable to speak the local language. Finally, you assign weights to airline fares, hotel prices, availability of tourist attractions, and ease of transportation.

In the end, France is selected for the following reasons. First, you are fluent in French because you took lessons in high school. Second, France scored the highest in tourist attractions (e.g., the Eiffel Tower, the Louvre, Notre Dame Cathedral), and ease of transportation (the national train system is well developed and not expensive). In this scenario, perception does not play much because your decision is driven by the summer vacation attributes.

The I→J→D pathway (analytical pathway) highlights that information and judgment are useful in pursuing a decision choice without taking into consideration experiences, strategies, or insights embedded in the perception function. That is, a structural methodology is used without any benefits from the perception function.

The analytical pathway is quite useful in detailing steps that include what types of information are to be included in the analysis function (*judgment*). In this function, an information source is weighted in relationship to other sources. Once these information sources are weighted, they can then be used to compare, contrast, or study before making a decision regarding selection or elimination of people, places, or things.

Given our technological and fast-moving society, computerization of this pathway can enable a consistent and comparable way of programming certain types of decision-making tasks. Of course, any information used in the analytical pathway must be deemed reliable and relevant, or faulty decision choices may be the outcome. Finally, the analytical procedure installed in the judgment function must be sound, reliable, and consistent.

I→P→D: Where Information Leads to Your Perception, Then to a Decision Choice

The Revisionist Pathway (I→P→D) highlights an unstructured environment in which you may use all available information to influence your perception before rendering a decision. In this particular situation, the information can be either complete or incomplete. However, due to the vagueness of the event, it becomes difficult for individuals to model the data according to rating, ranking, or ordering (Fig. 2.5). Therefore, the use of this pathway is highly dependent on changing information, resulting in a modification of how we perceive a situation.

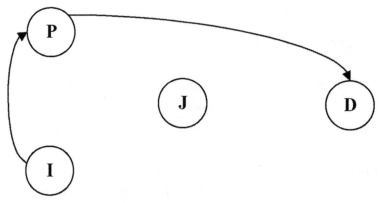

Figure 2.5. The Revisionist Pathway
I→P→D: Process thinking goes from Information influencing Perception and then to Decision.

The following represents examples for the *I→P→D* pathway.

I→P→D Pathway Example 1: Let's go back to the gathering of people at a party, the very important issue being discussed regarding pollution of major rivers, and the person with the severe stuttering problem who is leading the discussion. Everyone in the group knows that this person is the president of a major corporation and a graduate of Harvard University. This information would influence and overcome the perception of the person's speaking problem as merely a speech defect and not a lack of knowledge in a given area of concern.

Previously, when this example was discussed in the terms of decision-making based on perception alone, the people at the party did not analyze the president's education or knowledge about pollution (judgment). Hence, they allowed other information to influence their perceptions in making a decision to listen to and, perhaps, agree with the president's comments about pollution.

$I{\rightarrow}P{\rightarrow}D$ Pathway Example 2: Good physical conditioning is necessary for a person planning to take a demanding hike. If that person exercises regularly and is not overweight, then she may be in good enough shape to hike. Assume that an individual decides to go on a nature hike one weekend. She hires someone she believes to be a professional nature guide because she has no experience or knowledge about nature hiking. The guide is presently working in a store selling outdoor adventure supplies. He suggests supplies for her to purchase for the nature hike. She views him as a knowledgeable individual on this topic and therefore purchases the recommended supplies.

The *judgment* process is not used because she does not know how to compare, contrast, and/or analyze what supplies will be useful for her hiking trip. Rather, the *information* she acquired from the guide influenced how she viewed (*perception*) going on a nature hike, which led to her *decision choice*.

$I{\rightarrow}P{\rightarrow}D$ Pathway Example 3: It is a painfully simple truth that if a soldier falls in battle with a terrible injury, he will die if he does not receive medical attention promptly. On the ground, the fallen soldier has medical help ready at hand. But if he needs surgery, his best hope is to reach a nearby field surgical unit. A field surgeon might make frequent use of the information influencing perception to reach a decision. Before operating, the surgeon is given information on how the patient's injury occurred. This field unit could be a Combat Support Hospital (CSH).

The CSH's mission is to provide surgical support for the Army through advanced resuscitation and obligatory surgery. Under the cramped conditions and with time pressures, surgery and resuscitative procedures are prioritized to save lives and limbs. Wounds sustained in battle, and the manner in which they are managed, are very different from conventional practices.

The challenges involved in working in a CSH include having to deal with trauma injuries similar to automobile accidents. That is, a surgeon might notice burns from explosions, bullet wounds, and so on (*information*). The surgeon uses this type of information in surgery for a guideline of how to proceed, but must then rely on his or her instincts and experiences to frame the problem (*perception*) for lifesaving surgery (*decision choice*). Often the surgeon cannot afford the luxury of time for a thorough analysis (judgment) to be made.

The I→P→D pathway (Revisionist Pathway) depicts that adequate information set can assist in revising a person's previous way of framing or viewing a particular problem before making a decision. In this particular pathway, a detailed analysis (judgment function) is ignored when making a decision. This pathway can handle a degree of time pressure because a detailed analysis in the judgment function is not required for decision-making purposes. In addition, the revisionist pathway is suitable to environmental changes because this pathway allows information to update or change an individual's perception function before making a decision.

A subset of the I→P→D pathway includes the expedient pathway (P→D). This implies that a "quick" pathway to a decision is enhanced by the experience or expertise of the decision maker. Therefore, the revisionist pathway can use information to provide more awareness in the perception function to assist an individual's expertise in arriving at a decision.

P→I→J→D: Where Your Perception Influences Information That Leads to Judgment, Then to a Decision Choice

The Value-Driven Pathway (P→I→J→D) indicates how an individual's perceptual framing helps guide and select certain types of information used in the judgmental function. This pathway is influenced by information-processing limitations, complexity, and coherence between perception and the available information (Fig. 2.6). Hence, to take this pathway, you allow your perception to modify and select the information that will be analyzed for a decision.

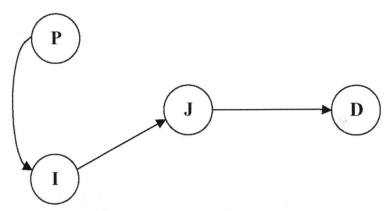

Figure 2.6. The Value-Driven Pathway
P→I→J→D: Process thinking starts with Perception influencing Information then to Judgment en route to Decision.

P→I→J→D Pathway Example 1: When voting in a national election, many people have already formed their perceptions of the candidates running for a public office. That is, they have already framed whether the person is moral, is likeable, and has good leadership skills. Even though information about the candidates can be found on the Internet, in television and radio ads, and in written pamphlet material, the voter must decide how reliable and relevant the information sources are.

However, many people voting for a political candidate allow their perceptions to influence what type of information they will believe and consider for analysis. Therefore, the voter has framed feelings (*perception*) about the political candidate and has determined what type of *information* to use in an analysis (*judgment*) about the candidates before making a *decision choice* on whom to vote for.

$P \rightarrow I \rightarrow J \rightarrow D$ Pathway Example 2: A very introverted and shy individual decides to attend the school dance. His attention is drawn toward a very attractive female student. He is confronted with a choice of whether or not he should ask her out on a date. This shy person has watched many romantic comedies in which an individual, similar to him, dates the woman he likes at the end of the movie.

Based on these types of movies, he is inclined to believe that he can succeed in dating her. He gathers more information about her and finds out that she's already dating the quarterback of the high school football team. In addition, her previous dates were all outstanding high school athletes.

Because of his framing (*perception*) of the problem, he filters out this *information* and only considers news about a possible breakup with the quarterback. He analyzes (*judgment*) the situation and asks her (*decision choice*) for a date, only to be turned down abruptly. In this scenario, the introverted and shy individual's perception was the dominating factor that guided him to filtering valuable information that contradicted his view of the possibility of dating her. This caused his judgment about his dating chances to be somewhat biased, resulting in an unfavorable decision.

$P \rightarrow I \rightarrow J \rightarrow D$ Pathway Example 3: Computer programmers tell a computer what to do by writing a program. Programmers typically follow descriptions prepared by systems analysts, who have carefully studied the task that the computer system is going to perform. These descriptions list the input required, the steps the computer must follow to process data, and the desired arrangement of the output.

Based on previous experience, a programmer believes that the program is not running correctly and will not produce the desired information. Her beliefs are based on her feelings that the previous computer programmer was incompetent. She prepares sample data that test every part of the program, and after trial runs, she reviews the results to see whether any errors were made. She finds errors, then changes and rechecks the program until it produces the correct results.

Hence, the computer programmer believed (*perception*) errors existed in the programming. To fix the problem, the programmer observed the source code, gaining *information* about how that part of the program functions. Next, careful analysis (*judgment*) was used to determine what would be the best course of action to take before rendering a *decision* on how to debug the program.

The P→I→J→D pathway (value-driven pathway) enables the perception function to influence the types of information to be selected for analysis in the judgment function before arriving at a decision choice. Great time pressures may prevent this pathway from being suitable for decision-making tasks. Also, the information set that is utilized is viewed as reliable and relevant for decision-making purposes.

A notable feature regarding the P→I→J→D pathway is that it includes the analytical pathway (I→J→D). That is, the perception function allows a modification to a preexisting format or procedure in solving problems or decision making. This modification represents a particular view or perspective by the decision maker. Typically, this view can represent a socially driven, culturally driven, or an individual particular way of understanding. Therefore, an analytical way of performing tasks can be enhanced by an individual's view of a situation.

I→P→J→D: Where Information Adjusts Your Perception That Leads to Judgment, Then to a Decision Choice

The Global Perspective Pathway (I→P→J→D) mode of operation assumes that the available information affects a decision maker's information search pattern and biases before an analysis (judgment) to rate, rank, or order information (Fig. 2.7).

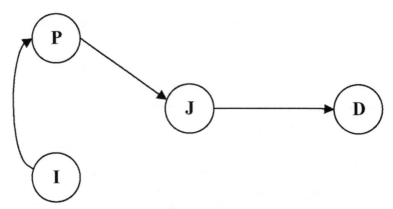

Figure 2.7. The Global Perspective Pathway
I→P→J→D: Process thinking begins with Information influencing
Perception then affecting Judgment to Decision.

I→P→J→D Pathway Example 1: If a person is considering plastic surgery, but does not know any doctors or friends who have previously undergone plastic surgery and could recommend good doctors, she would begin to research plastic surgeons because she has no previous perceptions of this type of doctor. After she locates doctors on the Internet, visits offices, and sees photographs of plastic surgeons' work, she would begin to form perceptions about each of the doctors.

The information collected about these doctors' work would influence how she perceives them. Perhaps, after several visits to a couple of surgeons' offices, she would increase the *information* quality to influence her *perception* of each doctor. She would then analyze both doctors' work and how she feels about each doctor. After completing her analysis (*judgment*), she would then make a final *decision* regarding the doctor who will perform her plastic surgery.

I→P→J→D Pathway Example 2: I have decided to travel to Lake Victoria in Uganda. It is the world's second-largest freshwater lake. I have no previous knowledge about this area of the world. Therefore, I search and gather information pertaining to the seasons of the year, climate, wildlife, tourist attractions, and safety precautions. I discover that this lake is about the size of the Republic of Ireland and forms the headwaters of the River Nile. I also learn that the three nations of Kenya, Tanzania, and Uganda share the waters of the lake. I examine more books, articles, and travel guide pamphlets on Lake Victoria and Uganda.

Based on this *information* I frame (*perception*) the best time for me to travel to this area. I begin to analyze which location in Uganda I deem to be the most appealing. Based on this analysis (*judgment*), I decide where and when to go on my first trip to Lake Victoria (*decision choice*).

$I \rightarrow P \rightarrow J \rightarrow D$ Pathway Example 3: Directors express ideas and create images in theater, film, radio, television, and other performing arts media. They interpret a writer's script to entertain, inform, or instruct an audience. They direct the work of the cast and crew because they are responsible for the artistic aspects of plays and scripts. They audition and select cast members, as well as conduct rehearsals. They are knowledgeable about the use of voice, movement, and acting techniques. In rehearsals, they use their knowledge to achieve the best possible performances from actors.

Directors usually approve scenery, costumes, and music. Let's say a movie director reads a movie script. The script (*information*) provides the director a basic idea of how to go about shooting a scene. However, the director's *perception* of actors' ability, stage setup, camera angle, and several other factors would affect her *judgment* of which scenes to select when deciding (*decision choice*) on the final scenes. The director analyzes the selection of the scenes to determine which ones theater audiences will view.

The $I \rightarrow P \rightarrow J \rightarrow D$ pathway (global perspective pathway) enables information sources to modify, enhance, or change the perception function, which influences analysis (judgment), before a decision is made. Because of the information demands on this pathway, time pressures may present problems for adoption. That is, it may take a considerable amount of time for informational sources to revise the perception function. Also, an unstable environment may cause the information set to become irrelevant.

The I→P→J→D pathway encompasses the ruling guide pathway (P→J→D pathway). That is, information provides support to improve on the rules by modifying the framing of a problem to be analyzed. Therefore, rules or laws are not blindly applied to a given situation without regard to changing environments or a better information channel.

Combining the Six Pathways

The six dominant pathways leading to a successful decision, as represented following, illustrate how forming our decision-making processes into a network can influence the choices that we make. The six pathways can be divided into four major groupings of no information, lack of perceptual influences, no detailed analysis (judgment), and complete use of the four concepts.

No Information
P→D
P→J→D

Lack of Perceptual Influences
I→J→D

No Detailed Analysis (Judgment)
P→D
I→P→D

Complete Use of the Four Concepts
P→I→J→D
I→P→J→D

Two of the pathways in the *process thinking model* ($P{\rightarrow}D$ and $P{\rightarrow}J$ ${\rightarrow}D$) downplay or ignore information sources (I). Part of the reason is related to the inadequacy of the reliability and relevance of information. That is, information could be compromised because of noisiness, incompleteness, errors, undifferentiated alternatives, and difficulty of interpretation.

Of course, time pressures, unstable environment, and the lack of expertise can contribute to these situations. The $I \rightarrow J \rightarrow D$ pathway highlights a more programmable and analytical approach to decision making. Perceptions (P) have very little influence in that information sources have been agreed on and are typically used in an unbiased, consistent, and systematic way. The $P{\rightarrow}D$ and $I \rightarrow P \rightarrow D$ pathways are routed around a more complex analysis (J) in making a decision choice. These conditions can be influenced greatly by expertise, instability of the environment, and time pressures.

Finally, only two of the six pathways employ all of the four major concepts. The pathways of $P{\rightarrow}I{\rightarrow}J{\rightarrow}D$ and $I{\rightarrow}P{\rightarrow}J{\rightarrow}D$ emphasize the interactions of all the major concepts, but in different combinations, in reaching a decision. The selection of one of these pathways depends on whether our perceptual framing (P) or information sources (I) will be the initiator or the driver of the remaining major concepts before arriving at a decision.

Summary

Your happiness, wealth, and dealings with people in general can improve by understanding which particular pathway is needed for a given situation. Depending on the circumstances, the six dominant pathways will use part or all of the major modes of decision making, that is, perception, information, judgment, and decision choice. These circumstances involve the degree of the individual's expertise, completeness of information sources, stability of the environment, and time pressures.

Six dominant pathways leading to a successful decision provide us with different ways of solving daily problems. The six major pathways are the Expedient Pathway (P→D), the Ruling Guide Pathway (P→J→D), the Analytical Pathway (I→J→D), the Revisionist Pathway (I→P→D), the Value-Driven Pathway (P→I→J→D), and the Global Perspective Pathway (I→P→J→D). Influencing the selection of these pathways is a combination of our experience level or expertise, time pressures, rapidly changing environment, and/or information being incomplete, noisy, difficult to interpret, or unmanageable to order in a reasonable way.

Finally, the six pathways can be separated into four significant groupings related to (1) no information, (2) lack of perceptual influences, (3) no detailed analysis (judgment), and (4) the use of all four concepts. These groupings can alert us to whether perception, information, and/or judgment may be used in decision-making tasks or solving problems.

CHAPTER 3

Why Framing Matters

> Judges have a very difficult time weighing and combining information, be it probabilistic or deterministic. To reduce cognitive strain, they resort to simplified strategies, many of which lead them to ignore or misuse relevant information.

—Paul Slovic and Sarah Lichtenstein, 1971

Our everyday activities in life are punctuated by our spiritual condition and state of mind. A spiritual force that directs us into good or bad activities drives our inner essence. Our mental state is shaped by our experiences, education, and training. Taken together, the spiritual condition and state of mind help shape how we frame a given situation. In all likelihood, no influence is as pervasive and powerful in its impact on decision making as perceptual framing.

Framing refers to the influence of (1) background context (that is, spiritual condition and state of mind) of a decision choice, and (2) the way in which the question is worded (frame). Also, our perceptual frames provide us with the ability to classify and categorize previous events stored in our memories. These events help mold the way we view our world. Events are formed from our earliest childhood recollections of our interactions with the environment. The environment covers family endeavors, economic status, religious practices, and social relations outside our home. We categorize and classify previous episodic events into memory layers to serve as a backdrop to be retrieved for any decision-making activities.

Unfortunately, sometimes our framing may not help us. Nobel Prize winner Daniel Kahneman and his colleague Amos Tversky (Kahneman, Slovic, and Tversky 1992) demonstrated how background context and the way something is worded might not result in the best decision. For example, advertisers, attorneys, government officials, lawyers, politicians, and public relations people are quite skilled at the use of the framing effect. Whenever anyone is presenting a case for anything, ask yourself how the issue might be reframed. Framed in a complementary way, do you still feel the same way about it?

The Nature of Decision Framing

A decision frame is an individual's stored knowledge that is used to solve a problem. This definition derives from theories of knowledge in cognitive science and artificial intelligence. For intelligent systems, including human beings, knowledge stored in memory is divided into partitions, and each partition is keyed to an environmental domain.

The meaning of a domain is specified by the knowledge in its particular partition. Memory includes representations of both specific experiences with various tasks (episodic memory) and general knowledge. Individuals' use prominent indicators that are present in a given situation (domain). This allows an individual to probe his/her memory in an attempt to locate an appropriate knowledge partition (frame) for that situation. The knowledge partition derives from individuals' past experiences with these or similar situations. The goal is to access this knowledge to (1) understand the current situation and (2) use that understanding to guide behavior in the current situation.

It is believed that there are two different kinds of frames. The *general frame* provides the context for the decision problem and serves to give coherence and structure to the problem by placing it within a broader perspective. The *specific frame* defines the problem itself in terms of the available information and issues and in terms of the broader perspective of the general frame.

Translated into a grocery shopping setting, the general frame consists of the shopper's knowledge applied to supermarkets. Further, this frame uses relevant information about store types and the environment in order to formulate a coherent picture about either existing or future environmental problems. Against this background impression of the supermarket and the environment, the shopper interprets information. That is, the manner in which the shopper deals with the details of supermarkets (the specific frame) is colored by the larger picture (the general frame) he or she has of the supermarket and the environment.

The Nature of Confidence and Expertise

Confidence is seen as a by-product, if you will, of individuals' perceptions and judgments involved in decision making. It is seen as a subjective evaluation of the reliability of the information that is being processed as well as an evaluation of the reliability of the process itself. In this view, confidence is a subjective index of decision precision. Confidence is typically higher in the correctness of decisions when individuals use well-structured, analytic process thinking than when they use less-formal processes, unless processing time was constrained by time pressures, in which case confidence is reduced.

Moreover, individuals who lack analytic skills or expertise are considerably less confident in decisions requiring even moderate analysis than are individuals who possess such skills. Hence, confident decisions reflect information properties and processing demands rather than the outcomes associated with decision alternatives. As such, confidence provides individuals with a measure of how much they should depend on the final decision, how likely it is to be accurate, and how much they should invest in its implementation.

Finally, so compelling are the influences of strategies on decision making that people demonstrate considerable overconfidence in decisions they make. This overconfidence appears to be reinforced by what is referred to as the *hindsight bias:* a tendency to falsely report that we would have accurately predicted an outcome—even if we had not been told about that outcome in advance. Clearly, "we knew it all the time." This after-the-fact style of decision making can result in poorer decisions because very little attention is directed to important information issues such as incompleteness, noisiness, undifferentiated alternatives, and difficult-to-interpret information.

Experts are considered to know more about their domain and appear to have more metaknowledge than novices. Experience helps individuals in that facts are programmed into specific rules for using them, and rules for controlling reasoning are composed and generalized. The first step for individuals is to use their knowledge to understand their environment. Uncertainty is related to an individual's opinion regarding his or her environment.

Experts as a group, contrasted with novices, may have less-mixed predictions about, let's say, patient recovery time after an Achilles tendon operation. Also, when comparing knowledge, experts are thought to be superior to novices in the areas of recall, categorization, and chunking of information. Experts produce better abstract representations of information and have a more cohesive representation of information than novices. They also show better clusters (meaningful groupings) of presented information, as well as greater reasoning capability.

Expertise plays two important roles in process thinking. First, expertise contributes to refinement and modification of reasoning processes in perception and judgment. That is, successful experiences reinforce already known rules or previous assumptions by experts. Unsuccessful experiences require reanalysis of the reasoning and knowledge that were used and modification of faulty rules and knowledge. Therefore, experience enhances problem solving and, in the process, turns novices into relatively more expert reasoners.

Second, individuals' experiences become the basis of later decisions. Analogies made to previous situations guide and focus subsequent decision making. Therefore, experts, when compared to novices, possess proficiencies not only in absorbing larger chunks of information and in encoding relatively more information but also in abstracting conceptual representations of the incoming information.

Experts' knowledge generally consists of general domain, subspecialty, and world knowledge. Individuals acquire *general domain knowledge* through instruction and experience in that domain. *Subspecialty knowledge* is acquired through formal instruction and experience and is specific to decision makers in that subspecialty area. *World knowledge* is accumulated through individual life experiences and instruction, and it is unlikely that all decision makers at a given experience level will possess it equally. Subspecialty knowledge is a key component of a task and, therefore, could present problems for novices.

Experts have a knowledge base for forecasting, that is, an assemblage of related facts. This personal knowledge base is a highly organized, formatted structure that experts access to solve problems. The knowledge base is analogous to a data structure. Thus, it is not a program; it is the universe of knowledge in memory that is constantly evolving and expanding.

Problem-solving activities represent perceptual sets of stimulation in the form of modeling how things ought to be or what things are, as well as action plans for resolution when the model is not met. Expert problem solvers have some commonality of approach when looking at long-term implications. Novice problem solvers tend to examine superficially and not to look at long-term implications of a situation. Rather, they adopt a strategy that tests a problem by accidental attempts at resolution. Should any clues surface, the accidental approach becomes more focused. This approach is also referred to as *similarity*, as on the surface the problem looks much like something that is familiar.

If the problem does not have a readily available solution, a more in-depth analysis is undertaken. This approach involves a more carefully planned and systematic attempt because it moves from short-term memory processing of the original problem to symbolic representation of the problem in long-term memory. Experts rely more on deeper features such as principles or procedures, whereas novices rely more on surface features or common factors.

Expertise in the Process Thinking Model

A variety of goals exists that affects how individuals interpret information and plan their actions. However, most of the goals that have been linked to perception and judgment are "imposed" by situations. For example, when individuals start a problem-solving exercise, they encode (*perceptual frame*), retrieve, and process information (*information set*) that influences how they interpret and analyze (*judgment*). If perceptual framing is found to affect individuals' judgment, then problems solved under time pressures should receive the closest scrutiny.

Because of ambiguities in the concept of expertise, it is difficult to identify who is an expert or who is more expert. Generally, professional expertise is thought to be acquired through training and experience, although the exact process by which good judgment is acquired is unknown.

Quite a few tasks are characterized either by uncertainty of information or outcome, by a concern for an individual's preference, or by both. Also, a criterion may not exist for determining whether a single *decision choice* is correct because the response is based, in part, on personal opinions or preferences. It is possible, however, to impose a logical structure on the task that defines the consistency of a set of individuals' responses. Therefore, process thinking is proposed, which may provide us with some insight into individuals' reasoning processes (Fig. 3.1).

In addition, the procedures by which decision makers formulate a *judgment* and the rules by which information is sorted and ranked vary (see chapter 5 for a detailed discussion regarding formulating a judgment). The processes of perception and judgment are sensitive to differences or deviations from present states (perception and information interacting), reference points (strategies and biases), and adaptation levels (perception and information processed through judgment).

In the view adopted here, decision choice is tied to perception, information, and judgment (Fig. 3.1). Information search may be systematic or unsystematic. Various strategies (compensatory and noncompensatory) are available for analysis (*judgment*). Finally, expert knowledge can have a significant effect on the judgment function. That is, a knowledge base acquired in a formal learning environment should affect individuals' judgment.

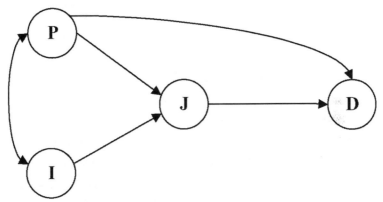

Figure 3.1. *Process Thinking Model*
Where P = perception, I = information, J = judgment, and D = decision choice.

Experts' Process Thinking

Experts' process thinking is influenced by two versions of the representative model. First is the directive that features of any fundamental cause must resemble the characteristics of the results to be explained. For example, an auditor may evaluate a company's method of estimating its profits as a stereotypical abstraction from similar companies.

Second is the condition that a cause must explain the effects of the type in question. For example, a superior court judge is assumed to make inferences on the basis of knowledge of the law and store these inferences as abstract concepts. Expert knowledge may aid decision makers' ability to combine information into larger organizational units for decision-making purposes. That is, their expert knowledge makes it easy for them to construct an overlaying conceptual structure, which in effect allows easy, frequent, and speedy access to a complex underlying body of knowledge make a decision choice.

When dealing with a large amount of knowledge, easy access to different subsets of information may make alternative information possible. Process thinking helps clarify how individuals select information and how, by a more in-depth analysis, they perform in the judgment function.

Experts appear to be better than novices at retrieval of knowledge, information search, and comprehension. Their use of directed information search strategies is based on preexisting knowledge structures. Apparently, experts are also better able than novices to search through less information and to make general interpretations of the data. Therefore, they are fairly good at building representations of situations.

On the other hand, novices process information sequentially because they lack these knowledge structures. Expertise requires a general understanding of the overall sequence of forecasting audit activities. That is, experts are able to implement a knowledge base of an assemblage of related facts in budget forecasting. Expert problem solvers tend to have some commonality of approach when solving problems. In particular, experts' representations seem to be larger, taking into account more of the available information. Novices, on the other hand, tend not to probe deeply and not to look at the long-term implications of the forecasted budget.

The model differences between experts and novices strengthened support for expertise in forecasting events. For the experts' model, it is apparent that expert knowledge, or some unidentified antecedents, is contributing significantly to their judgments. The use of expert knowledge can shape the way individuals make their choices. Process thinking can be used to capture your knowledge and different functions of processing before arriving at a decision.

Selected Process Thinking Strategies

People implement strategies to function in a systematic manner, especially when confronted with what we believe to be similar events. Automatic strategies and information processing strategies are involved in most decision choices. Errors, biases, and context-dependent strategies may result from mental mechanisms of which decision makers are largely unaware and may have a direct or indirect impact on decision choice.

We also use other perceptual strategies. For example, belief bias and confirmation bias, as well as the anchoring/adjustment, representation, and availability are some of the strategies used by individuals (Table 3.1).

Table 3.1 *Strategies and Biases*

➤ Hindsight bias ----➤ Ignore present information available at the time.

➤ Belief bias ----➤ Interference to new information (dogma).

➤ Confirmation bias ----➤ Selective framing of a problem whereby one tends to examine what confirms one's beliefs.

➤ Anchoring/adjustment ----➤ Judgments are frequently influenced by a perceptual starting point.

➤ Representative ----➤ We frequently perceive the likelihood of an event based on the similarity to the population from which it is drawn (i.e., our view of most typical situations).

➤ Availability ----➤ Refers to estimates of frequency or probability that are made on the basis of how easily examples come to mind.

The *belief-bias* effect resonates because of our perceptual frame locked in on a prior belief. That is, the belief in an idea, concept, or thing can outweigh other relevant and reliable information.

Confirmation bias refers to selective framing of a problem whereby you tend to examine only what confirms your beliefs. In addition, you ignore or undervalue the relevance of what contradicts your beliefs. For example, if you believe that during a sunny day there is an increase in highway accidents, you will take notice of highway accidents on a sunny day but be inattentive to the accidents on a rainy day. A tendency to do this over time unjustifiably strengthens your belief in the relationship between sunny days and accidents.

The Anchoring and Adjustment Strategy

This particular strategy relates to judgments that are often influenced by a perceptual starting point and adjustments to that starting point. This strategy is usually related to facts and figures that can influence judgments. Notice the difference in your perception if I indicate that you can save $50 on the cost of a cellular telephone by purchasing it at a certain store versus telling you that you can save $50 on the cost of a high-tech television by going to a certain merchandising store.

Your perception is anchored to the cost of these items. A $50 savings on a cellular telephone that costs $100 is perceived as considerable compared to $50 savings on a high-tech television that may cost about $4,000. However, in terms of your personal finances, $50 is $50, precisely the same amount, no matter how it occurs. If you want it in one situation, you should want it equally in the other.

Representative Strategy

This strategy points to the fact that we frequently judge the likelihood of an event based on the similarity to the population from which it is drawn. Similarity in these situations is often defined in terms of prototype—our view of the most typical situation.

Consider the set of results (heads and tails) from a coin toss experiment. Most individuals perceive that the sequence H H H T T T is much too normal to be a random event; it doesn't conform to our view that for an event to be random, so it must have a certain irregularity about it. Statistically, however, the sequence H H H T T T has the same probability as, say, H T T H T H.

Sample Size and Representativeness

Individuals often try to include probability and statistics in their thinking and decision making. Unfortunately, the probabilities and statistical outcomes we use are often based on large sample sizes, despite the fact that our decision making involves small sample sizes.

For example, you have tossed a coin nine times, and it has come up heads all nine times. On the tenth toss, is it more likely to come up a head or a tail? Most individuals believe that it's more likely to come up a tail. Someone might say, "After all, it's come up heads nine times in a row. Undoubtedly, it will come up tails next—it's the law of averages." As a matter of fact, the probabilities of a head or a tail on the tenth toss are equal (.50). The incorrect conclusion that a tail is more likely is based on what is known as the *small-sample fallacy*, which assumes that small samples will be representative of the population from which they are selected.

The small-sample fallacy could be, in part, one of the explanations for the strong stereotypes we form of other ethnic and racial groups. Diversity and multiculturalism are effective means of eliminating stereotyping based on the small-sample fallacy, in that they permit us to become acquainted with large numbers of individuals from other groups.

Base Rate and Representativeness

Base rate indicates how often an element (or event) occurs in the population. That is, you know that the probability of drawing such an item is equal to the number of such items divided by the total number of elements in the population. So persuasive is representativeness and its linked stereotyping that we usually ignore base-rate information and base our decisions on representativeness. This is known as the *base-rate fallacy.* Take into account the following personality sketch of an imaginary person named Steve, which appeared in a study by Kahneman and Tversky (1973, p. 241):

> "Steve is very shy and withdrawn, invariably helpful, but with not much interest in individuals or in the world of reality. A meek and tidy soul, he has a need for order and structure, and a passion for detail."

Subjects were asked to read these two sentences and then to judge Steve's occupation from a list of possibilities that included farmer, salesperson, airline pilot, librarian, and physician. Knowledge of base rates would suggest that there are a greater number of salespeople in the world than there are librarians, leading to the conclusion that Steve is, in fact, most likely a salesperson. Yet, because the description corresponds to our stereotype of the librarian, most people think that he is a librarian. As evidenced in studies by Amos Tversky and Daniel Kahneman (1974), such errors occur even when the base rate is given.

The Conjunction Fallacy and Representativeness

If two events occur together or separately, the conjunction, where they overlap or have something in common, cannot be more likely than the chance of either of the two individual events. However, decision makers often forget this and assign a higher chance to combination events. That is, we erroneously associate quantity of events with quantity of probability.

What if I ask you which has the greater probability in a single draw from a deck of cards, getting a diamond or obtaining a diamond that is also a picture card? Most individuals have no difficulty with this problem. They correctly reason that of the 52 cards in the deck, 13 are diamonds, but only 4 are both diamonds and picture cards. Because 13/52 (1/4) is greater than 4/52, clearly the probability of getting a diamond is greater than that of getting a diamond that is also a picture card. However, consider the following presentation based on an experiment by Tversky and Kahneman (1983):

When describing the attributes of a person, subjects consistently categorized "Bank teller and feminist" significantly higher than "Bank teller." Perhaps especially startling is that statistical knowledge had no effect on the outcome. The preceding item was provided to three groups: The first was a statistically naive group of undergraduates; the second, a group of first-year graduate students who had taken one or more statistics courses; and the third, a group of doctoral students in a decision science program who had taken several advanced courses in probability and statistics (labeled statistically naive, intermediate knowledge, and statistically sophisticated, respectively).

Most individuals committed what is described as the *conjunction fallacy*: They thought the probability of the conjunction is greater than the probability of the basic event. This means, given the card example earlier, the likelihood of drawing a diamond picture card is greater than the probability of drawing a simple diamond. Again, the stereotype of the feminist leads us to this erroneous conclusion in decision making.

The Availability Strategy

The availability strategy refers to estimates of frequency or probability that are made on the basis of how easily examples come to mind. Individuals judge frequency by assessing whether relevant examples can be easily retrieved from memory or whether this memory retrieval requires great effort. Because availability is typically correlated with an objective frequency of an event, the use of this strategy usually leads to valid conclusions. However, because several factors that strongly influence memory retrieval are not correlated, they can distort availability in a way that leads to erroneous conclusions.

Amos Tversky and Daniel Kahneman (1973) performed a classic study that defined the availability strategy. In this study, subjects were asked to consider two general categories of words; those with the letter *k* in the first position and those with the letter *k* in the third position. The subjects were then asked to estimate the relative proportions of each kind of word. The researchers found that people guess that about twice as many words have the letter *k* in the first position relative to those that have *k* in the third position. Actually, about twice as many words have *k* in the third position.

The results indicate that we are very familiar with considering words in terms of their initial letters and rarely reflect on words in terms of their third letters. Accordingly, retrieval of words beginning with *k* is much easier—many more are available—than words with *k* in the third position. The availability and effortlessness of retrieval lead to the illusory conclusion that many more begin with *k*. Because availability is very much associated with retrieval, it is highly influenced by variables related to memory such as recency and familiarity.

Recency and Availability

Because memory for events typically deteriorates with time, more recent occurrences are recalled more accurately. Because recent items are more available, we judge them to be more likely than they really are.

Familiarity and Availability

Familiarity can also enhance availability, thereby distorting our thinking. Overall, events that are highly familiar lead us to overestimate their likelihood relative to less-familiar events. For example, emphasis in the news (what's newsworthy, what's not) explains the compelling influence of journalism. Murders get reported, but random acts of kindness rarely do. Hence, it is easy to overestimate deaths from murders relative to deaths from disease. Recency and familiarity, then, are likely to pollute a strategy that otherwise works pretty well.

Illusory Correlation and Availability

Another influence on availability is illusory correlation. Correlation refers to a relation between two variables (that is, variables that covary). In a positive relationship, when one variable increases, the other does also, whereas in a negative relationship the variance is in opposite directions (when one increases, the other decreases). An illusory correlation refers to the belief that a correlation exists when it does not. Illusory correlation is believed to be the cornerstone of many stereotypes and prejudices (for example, certain racial or ethnic groups, genders, or body types are lazy, dumb, violent, unemotional, overly emotional, or have rhythm).

Illusory correlations may arise due to the selective information we include regarding other individuals. We retain the information that confirms our stereotype and disregard disconfirming information (generally as an exception to the rule). In learning prejudices from parents and peers, they provide us with a frame or schema for incorporating information from our social experience. The schema leads us to focus on the attributes of others that confirm the stereotype.

The Simulation Strategy and Availability

A special case of availability is called the simulation strategy. That is, on some occasions we need to make decisions in the absence of prior experience. The simulation strategy refers to the ease with which we can imagine a situation or event.

Table 3.2 *Representative and Availability Strategies*

➤ **Influences on Representative Heuristic** ------➤

Sample size
   Individuals try to include probability and
   statistics into their thinking. However, our
   decision-making involves small sample sizes.

Base rate
   We usually ignore base-rate information and base our
   decisions on representativeness.

Conjunctive fallacy
   The probability of the conjunction is greater than
   the probability of the basic event.

➤ **Influences on Availability** ------➤

Recency
   More recent events are recalled more accurately.

Familiarity

   Events that are highly familiar lead us to
   overestimate their likelihood relative to events
   that are less familiar.

Illusory correlation
   Refers to the belief that a correlation exists when
   it, in fact, does not.

Simulation heuristic
   There are occasions when we need to make decisions
   in the absence of prior experience.

Summary

Framing can help individuals shape and aid their judgments regarding describing and predicting events. This approach to individuals' decision making emphasizes the function of framing the problem and the role of confidence in process thinking. We assume that the coherence of the general frame, derived from background and information, contributes to a feeling of understanding and confidence. Further, confidence appears to grow from understanding, and they both contribute to the specific frame of a task and are reflected in evaluation (and confidence in that evaluation) of descriptions and predictions of events. This evaluation appears to drive the decision, whereas confidence in the evaluation appears to drive confidence in the decision.

A general frame for tasks is generated by what is known initially about the environment, together with information procured, to produce a broader understanding, to create a specific frame for the problem itself. For example, the specific frame is generated through application of generally accepted auditing procedures that produce further information about the client and result in an evaluation of the fairness of the client's financial statements. The evaluation is then used to generate a decision about the kind of opinion to be issued. Paralleling this is the individuals' confidence in their understanding of the information that has been generated, their evaluations, and their decisions. Confidence is engendered by information, but it underlies an expert's willingness to use that information in important decisions, particularly the ultimate audit decision about the opinion to be issued.

An individual's perception and judgment processes are partly "objective" and partly "subjective." That is, the information itself can best be thought of as objective, in that trained persons would tend to agree with it. However, the *interpretation* of the information, both general and specific, is subjective, as are the feelings of confidence they engender. Therefore, both objective and subjective components are necessary parts of process thinking; to fail to understand either is to fail to understand the process itself.

CHAPTER 4

Why Information May Not Be Enough

"I go with my gut feeling when I have acquired information somewhere in the range of 40% to 70%."

—General Colin L. Powell
(My American Journey, 2001)

Every day in our lives, we are confronted with choices that are either simple or complex. Generally we arrive at our decisions based on the situation and our previous experiences. *Process thinking* emphasizes four major concepts that are part of our decision-making tasks. They are *perception (P),* or framing and assessing a situation, *information (I)* that is available at the present time, *judgment (J)* or analysis of possible factors that are rated or ranked, and the *decision choice (D).* At least two of these four major elements will be present in making a decision, and when combined, they will fall into one of six pathways to arrive at a decision. These pathways are

(1) The Expedient Pathway   P→D
(2) The Ruling Guide Pathway   P→J→D

(3) The Analytical Pathway   I→J→D
(4) The Revisionist Pathway   I→P→D
(5) The Value-Driven Pathway   P→I→J→D
(6) The Global Perspective Pathway   I→P→J→D

These pathways, when taken individually, can represent only one-sixth, or approximately 16.7 percent, of accountable explanations, descriptions, or predictions about our decisions. Therefore, if we rely on just one pathway exclusively for our decision-making purposes, then on the average 83.3 percent (*which represents the other major five pathways*) of possible better ways to arrive at a decision are neglected. When we forget or do not use the other pathways, we could set ourselves up for disaster. It is interesting to note that the Analytical Pathway (*I→J→D*) is typically considered to be the most objective and rigorous means to a decision. This pathway, *I→J→D*, highlights the fact that no biases (i.e., perceptual framing) can creep into our analysis. When we are asked about how we arrived at a decision, we often point to the process of the *I→J→D* pathway. Assuming that this is the correct pathway, let us view potential problems with the so-called analytical and programmatic decision-making process of the *I→J→D* pathway.

Unfortunately, the analytical and programmatic decision-making process does not guide us to rate incomplete or noisy information, inadequate understanding, and undifferentiated alternatives. It does not tell us how to rate alternatives when the outcome on a particular event is uncertain. Further, it has not provided rules for determining the optimal alternative under uncertainty. For example, we tend to identify important attributes or properties from an information set. To use an analytical and programmatic decision-making process for a particular set of information, the concepts of *information*, *events*, and *uncertainty* must be known and recognized. This information set can be viewed as precise or vague.

Information is precise if it can be interpreted in exactly one way. Information is imprecise or vague if it is not clearly defined or cannot be understood in at least one precise way. In addition, *events* or objects are vague if they cannot be completely ordered. For example, if we cannot order Company A, Company B, and Company C from best to worst management team, then these objects are vague.

Uncertainty can also be considered as precise or vague. For example, let us consider rolling a die and calculating the probability that the number 5 will appear on top. A die (plural: dice) is a small cube—a square, box-shaped solid with a different number of spots on each of its six sides.

The probability that a rolled die will display the number 5 is a *precise* uncertainty of 1/6. Also, this is an illustration of a "problem-solving" outcome when we can calculate an exact probability of occurrence. Unfortunately, in most real-world problems, the precise uncertainty for each outcome is not known. Calculating the probability of rainfall two years from now in Rome, Italy, on four days in June requires *vague* uncertainties. Most financial and investment problems are of this variety, and the outcomes are classified as "decision-making" problems.

Referring to the eight cells of Table 4.1, we can summarize the concepts of event, uncertainty, and information. Cell 2, in which precise uncertainty about precise events is represented by vague information, might occur in determining that DaimlerChrysler Corporation's stock price will outperform a newly started automobile corporation without a profit history. The information may be vague regarding management and the financial statements of the two companies if it is not completely available to us. However, we may still be able to determine the preciseness of uncertainty and the event based on our knowledge regarding DaimlerChrysler Corporation and the 30-year history of start-up automobile companies' stock prices.

Cells 1 and 3 include both types of uncertainty regarding precise events. These cells depict the traditional probabilistic approach of an analytical and programmatic decision model. From an investment banker's perspective, however, cell 4 is more appropriate when information (vague) is gathered from unaudited or incomplete financial statements and it is difficult to assess the probability of whether the stock price will double for a company in the next year (precise event).

Under the analytical and programmatic pathway, cells 5, 6, 7, and 8 can never occur because the events must be precise to determine their rank, order, and so forth. For example, uncertainty about a vague accounting event pertaining to what month a company will distribute dividend checks can never be precise when compared to three other companies without a history of distributing dividend checks. Ordering these companies in terms of dividend payments is very difficult.

In other words, it is incorrect to apply an analytical and programmatic pathway decision model to vaguely defined events. Hence, an analytical and programmatic approach can at best account for only 50 percent of all possible conditions as represented in Table 4.1. Therefore, it is necessary to use a model that incorporates and addresses all the conditions in Table 4.1.

Table 4.1 **UNCERTAINTY x EVENT TYPE x INFORMATION PRESENTED**

	Precise Uncertainty		Vague Uncertainty	
	Precise Information	Vague Information	Precise Information	Vague Information
Precise Events	1	2	3	4
Vague Events	5	6	7	8

Because an analytical and programmatic approach can only account for (at best) 50 percent of all possible situations, it is necessary to expand this model to capture the other 50 percent.

In addition, when information is viewed as vague or imprecise, it may not be relevant and reliable. For example, if a situation calls for exact numbers to open a combination lock, then vague or inexact numbers may not be sufficient. Therefore, if information has to be exact, then only 2/8 (25 percent) of the cells are useful. Recall that cells 5 and 7 (precise information) are not reliable and relevant because the events are vague or imprecise. That is, if the events are vague, then information loses its differentiating quality. For example, we may not be able to differentiate whether Brand ABC washing machines are better or worse than Brand XYZ washing machines.

Process thinking provides organization and different distinctive functions during information gathering and analysis before arriving at a decision choice. Although process thinking has organization, it also allows enough flexibility for an individual to recognize the arrangement of the four major functions of perception, information, judgment, and decision choice in sustaining future actions. *Process thinking* depicts the interactions of these four major concepts of decision making and problem solving.

Figure 4.1 illustrates how the process of an individual's decision choice is made. If perceived causality is an important determinant of how an individual represents a problem and uses the information, it is necessary to know what determines the perception of causality in *process thinking*. Because decision makers typically process information subjectively, it is interdependent with perception in the model. The situational information and the decision maker's prior expectations or beliefs about the information are relevant to perceiving the degree of coherence between them. The interdependency and redundancy of perceptual effects and presented information affect the kinds of judgment and strategies that individuals use.

In *process thinking*, information also affects judgment. For example, information that is stored and retrieved from memory affects decision makers' evaluations of investment or credit portfolios. Typically, before an individual can make a decision, that individual encodes the information and develops a representation for the problem. Finally, perception and judgment can affect decision choice. Errors, biases, and context-dependent strategies may result from decision-making procedures of which decision makers are largely unaware and may have a direct impact on decision choice. The strategies of judgment that influence decision choice are under an individual's deliberate control.

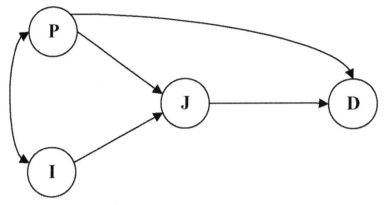

Figure 4.1. *Process Thinking Model*
Where P = perception, I = information, J = judgment, and D = decision choice.

Summary

Information has varying degrees of relevancy and reliability that can be viewed in eight different ways. Information used by individuals is shaped by its uncertainty of occurrence (precise or vague), nature or kind of information (precise or vague), and comparability of events or objects (precise or vague). Uncertainty of occurrence is *precise* when an accurate probability can be calculated or projected.

Process thinking is adaptable to a variety of situations. The process thinking approach is applicable to financial and investment situations that have a closed solution format (precise events), such as *"problem-solving"* types, as well as those of a *"decision-making"* nature (vague events). In addition, because of the complexities inherent in financial and investment analysis, it is helpful for our perception and judgment to be guided in selecting, processing, and analyzing the appropriate information for analysis. In passing, *process thinking* can serve as a means to benefit individuals in their selective processing when confronted with a sea of information.

CHAPTER 5

Judgment and Decision Choice

A quick and sound judgment, good commonsense, kind feeling, and an instinctive perception of character, in these are the elements of what is called tact, which has so much to do with acceptability and success in life.

—Charles Simmons

There are countless times in individuals' lives when they have to make decisions. People often make quite a few decisions by analyzing the problem as well as considering other alternatives.

Judgments are heavily influenced by individuals' strategy preferences. When a selection will yield potential consequences across more than one alternative, attribute, or dimension, the individual must prioritize to select a single alternative. The different strategies or "decision rules" used in reaching a decision based on perceptual frames and information can be classified into the two groups of *conflict confronting* and *conflict avoiding*. Conflict-confronting strategies are compensatory strategy techniques. That is, they allow a trade-off of a low value on one dimension or attribute against a high value on another. For example, during a compensatory strategy, an individual would be prepared to accept an automobile with an expensive high-performance engine against its low gas mileage.

Compensatory decisions are rational. However, individuals generally are faced with time pressures, lack expertise, and/or do not have enough information to make compensatory decisions. Collecting and comparing all the necessary information is simply too labor intensive. Therefore in contrast, conflict-avoiding strategies are noncompensatory strategy techniques that can save time and effort because they do not allow trade-offs. For instance, that same individual might decide that purchasing an automobile that drives smoothly is very important and that a high-maintenance automobile would not be considered, no matter how attractive the automobile was in other aspects. Thus, no high-maintenance-cost vehicles would be purchased.

The noncompensatory strategy models imply "satisficing" choice behavior and, as such, have the advantages and disadvantages of this strategy. Satisficing (introduced by Herbert Simon in his Models of Man in 1957) is an alternative to optimization for situations with multiple and competitive objectives in which one gives up the idea of obtaining a "best" solution. In this method an individual sets lower limits for the various objectives that, if attained, will be sufficient. Next, the individual seeks a solution that will exceed these limits. Problem solving presents too many uncertainties and conflicts in values for there to be any hope of obtaining an optimization; hence, it is more reasonable to set out to do "well enough."

Compensatory Models

In the compensatory model, it is assumed that each dimension (for example, cost of vehicle, brand name, or low or high maintenance) can be measured on a scale (implicitly at least) and given a weight reflecting its relative importance. The evaluation of each alternative is then the sum of the weighted values on the dimension. That is, value of alternative = sum of (relative weight × scale value) of all dimensions.

For example, in evaluating a television one, you may give the weights of 0.30, 0.50, and 0.20 to price, size, and brand name, respectively. For television two, you provide the weights of 0.30, 0.30, and 0.40 to price, size, and brand name, respectively. The weights represent the importance you place on these three items. Also assume that the scale values are 1.00, 2.00, and 3.00 for price, size, and brand name, respectively. The scale weights are standardized to compare with other types of televisions. Hence, for television one the value is $(0.30 \times 1.00) + (0.50 \times 2.00) + (0.20 \times 3.00) = 1.90$. For television two the value is $(0.30 \times 1.00) + (0.30 \times 2.00) + (0.40 \times 3.00) = 2.10$. A decision choice is then made by reference to the alternative having the greatest value, which is television two.

There are weaknesses inherent to this type of analysis. As a description of the choice processes, the compensatory model is often inadequate. It implies a process of explicit calculations and the trading off of dimensions, which, when there are many alternatives and dimensions, is not feasible for unaided judgment. Also, even when the number of dimensions and alternatives is small, individuals may still avoid conflict-type strategies. Two of the possible derivations of the compensatory model are the additive difference model and the ideal point model.

In the additive difference model, the decision maker is assumed to evaluate the differences between the two alternatives on a dimension-by-dimension basis and then to aggregate the differences to see which of the alternatives is favored by the aggregate net difference. However, it is important to note that individuals have quite different decision strategies. That is, identical outcomes can result from quite different processes.

In the ideal point model, an individual has in mind an ideal alternative, and each choice is evaluated on the basis of how it varies from the ideal. That is, the individual has a representation of what the "ideal" alternative would be. Given that certain alternatives are close to the ideal on some dimensions, effort needs to be expended only on considering the remaining dimensions. The ideal point model only predicts the same choice alternatives as the compensatory model if the distances from the ideal point on different dimensions are evaluated in a linear manner.

Noncompensatory Models

Four examples of noncompensatory models are the conjunctive, disjunctive, lexicographic, and elimination-by-aspects formulations. The conjunctive model is one in which an individual sets certain cutoff points on the dimensions such that any alternative that falls below a cutoff is eliminated. For example, in a loan decision, three primary criteria relate to a potential borrower's income, debt, and total assets. The decision maker could decide not to make a loan to any loan applicants who fail to meet certain levels on all criteria.

The disjunctive model is used when an individual will permit a low score on a dimension provided there is a very high score on one of the other dimensions. In other words, in the disjunctive model, the applicant would be evaluated according to his/her best attribute, regardless of the level on the other attributes. To continue the loan-making example, an applicant could have a very low net income, but the loan officer would be prepared to overlook that aspect provided the applicant had an abundance of assets.

The lexicographic model is implemented when the first action of the decision maker is to consider the relative importance of the dimensions and make an initial comparison on the basis of the most important dimension. Assume, for example, that the managers of a bank are deciding which type of loan portfolio (e.g., agriculture, real estate) should be considered for the investment of additional loans. They should target their loan efforts, focusing on return on investment, riskiness, and average length of loans outstanding. If two or more loan portfolios are equally "best" on return on investment, the second most important dimension should be used to distinguish between them. If that is insufficient, the third criterion should be used, and so on.

The elimination-by-aspect model is related to the linear model and is also sequential in nature. It assumes that alternatives consist of a set of aspects or characteristics. At each function of the process, an aspect that is a dimension is selected according to a probabilistic scheme (based on the presence of aspects among the remaining alternatives), and alternatives that do not include the aspect are eliminated. One of the weaknesses of the elimination-by-aspect-model is that the alternatives are eliminated before thorough consideration of their merits.

The four noncompensatory strategies (which do not allow for trade-offs) include the conjunctive rule, which eliminates choices possessing at least one attribute that falls outside a predetermined "acceptable" range, and the disjunctive rule, which values each choice according to its most desirable attribute. The next two represent the lexicographic strategy, in which the decision maker chooses the most important choice dimension, compares all alternatives on the basis of that dimension. Next, in the event that any alternatives remain, goes on to compare the next-most-important choice dimension, and so on; and elimination by aspects, a probabilistic version of lexicographic choice. The way in which a choice is framed will be a significant factor in determining which of the strategies will be used.

Finally, an important distinction among individuals' decision-making strategies is the degree to which they are compensated. A compensatory strategy is one in which a good value on one attribute can compensate for a poor value on another. A compensatory strategy thus requires explicit trade-offs among attributes. If a good score on one attribute can make up for a bad score on another, an individual is said to be using a compensatory evaluation.

In a noncompensatory strategy, a good value on the attribute cannot make up for a poor value on another. We can view compensatory versus noncompensatory as a bipolar dimension to identify decision-making strategies. Certain noncompensatory strategies (e.g., lexicographic and elimination-by-aspects strategies) fall at one extreme of the dimension, and certain compensatory strategies (for example, equal weight and adding weights to our strategies) fall at the opposite extreme.

Noncompensatory evaluation strategies can take many forms. Their common characteristic is that the presence or strength of one attribute cannot compensate for a weakness or absence of another attribute. If "low price" is the most important attribute, an individual will not purchase a more expensive product, even if it has many desirable features. Alternatively, if a brand does not meet some minimum requirement for an attribute, such as a snack being at least minimally nutritious, an individual might simply eliminate that brand. Sometimes individuals simply purchase what they bought last time.

Decision Choice Influence by Framing and Analysis

Decision choice involves selection of the best alternative solution or course of action. During this phase, an individual should use his or her abilities to ensure that the decision is carried out according to guidance. There are three types of decisions: choices, evaluations, and constructions. In a choice situation, an individual is confronted with a well-defined set of alternatives, and the usual task is to choose one of them. Evaluations, on the other hand, represent indications of worth for an individual's alternatives. Finally, constructions are decisions in which an individual tries to assemble the most satisfactory alternative possible. Typically, these constructions are driven by perceptual framing of the problem, which provides results based on biases, strategies, or framing of past events related to the problem at hand.

Summary

The different strategies utilized in your judgment based on perceptual frames and information can be classified into the two groups of compensatory and noncompensatory. In compensatory decisions, when the final values for dimensions are calculated, equal or higher value positive dimensions can compensate for negative dimensions. For instance, a computer that costs $250 more (negative dimension) may ultimately be the better choice because it performs more efficiently (positive dimension).

However, typically individuals make noncompensatory decisions because they don't collect all the relevant information systematically, fall short in considering the relative importance of various dimensions, or do not trade off the benefits of some dimensions against the weaknesses of others. Noncompensatory strategies are fundamentally shortcuts in the compensatory strategy process to make the judgment function easier. For instance, in the computer example given earlier, individuals may simply not collect information on all the relevant attributes. They may consider price but not computer efficiencies.

Process thinking allows us to understand and explain the influence of perception and information on the judgment function. The more we rely on our perceptual framing of a situation, the less we rely on the information set. If this is the case, we will probably use more of a noncompensatory strategy. However, the more analytical and information-seeking we become in our analysis, the higher the likelihood of using a compensatory strategy.

CHAPTER 6

P→D
The Expedient Pathway

> Having harvested all the knowledge and
> wisdom we can from our mistakes and
> failures, we should put them behind us and
> go ahead, for vain regretting interferes with
> the flow of power into our own personalities.
>
> —Edith Johnson

In chapter 4, it was pointed out that information could be divided into eight cells. Only two of these cells (25 percent) provide us with reliable and relevant information. When information need not be too exacting, only four of these cells need to be used. Therefore, at most, 50 percent (4/8) of the time information can be deemed useful for decision-making purposes.

However, between 25 and 50 percent of the time, information should be enhanced by other factors. These factors typically arise from our perceptual framing (P) of the situation. Although perceptual framing is strongly influenced by time pressures, incomplete information, and instability of the environment, it remains our "beaming light" at the other end of the tunnel. This so-called beaming light shines in relation to our experiences. Despite the fact that our experiences may be at times biased or misdirected, hopefully it can provide the missing puzzle pieces due to incomplete information sources.

The pathway from $P \rightarrow D$ can serve us well when we have limited time to make a decision. Time limitation can be a result of other things on our mind competing for our attention. Our knowledge about performing a particular task can also lead us down this particular pathway. Finally, not using information effectively as a result of its incompleteness, noise interference, or interpretation problems can promote the use of this pathway. This pathway provides the most efficient way to a decision. That is, it represents the shortest distance, compared to the other five pathways to a decision. A great deal of attention is given to the "P," or perception.

Perception represents how we *frame* our environment based on our experiences, which are augmented by our education and economic, political, and social ways of life. In addition, perception also is shaped by our ways of memory searches or strategies.

Further, our emotions and biases can influence how we frame a particular situation and order from memory the events we believe to be important. These search patterns enable us to take shortcuts through an immense memory filled with catalogs upon catalogs of our daily activities, lessons learned, episodic events, and more. Perception assists us in categorizing and classifying events in our memory to take us down one of six pathways to make a decision. For the $P \rightarrow D$ pathway, a great deal of emphasis is placed on how we frame our world, and little emphasis is placed on the available information set (I), as indicated in Figure 6.1.

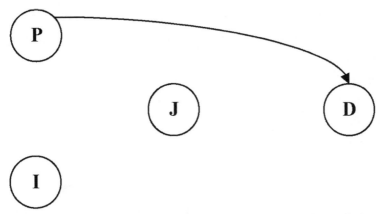

Figure 6.1. *P→D* Decision Is Made Based on Perception Only.

Example 1: One day you decide to shop for fruit at the supermarket nearest to your house. You arrive at the supermarket around seven o'clock in the evening and proceed to purchase some oranges and apples. When approaching the checkout lane, you suddenly remember that you intended to buy a box of cereal. You look at your watch, and it shows 7:15 PM. In fifteen minutes, a local television station will broadcast a local championship sporting event.

You do not want to miss the game, so you hurry to select a box of cereal. There is not much time to search; hence, you scan the cereal shelf for Corn Flakes or Granola. Unfortunately, there is neither Corn Flakes nor Granola in sight, but you do see a box of Raisin Bran. Though you do not consume Raisin Bran on a regular basis, you select it for purchase. You believe that Raisin Bran provides sufficient nutrients for your daily needs. Besides, as the commercial says, "Raisin Bran is very good for you." Also, the box of Raisin Bran is close and convenient. With limited time on hand, you take a box of Raisin Bran. You have made a decision choice almost spontaneously, without proceeding with a detailed analysis of the situation.

Example 2: Perception to decision choice could entail a degree of expertise as applied to a situation without reliable information. Informed perceptions could help prevent a disaster from occurring. For instance, you smell something burning on your stove. There is no time to go through a detailed thought process. Your immediate response is to turn off the stove. After you turn off the stove, you discover that boiling water in a pot containing two eggs has evaporated.

Example 3: Going directly from *perception* to *decision choice* could be very risky because there is no reliable and relevant information to consider. For example, two individuals apply for a middle management position in a large company. Both have similar experience and qualifications, but one is raggedly dressed, and the other is dressed very professionally. The one who is dressed professionally is more likely to get the job based on the employer's visual impression alone.

Example 4: I am walking across a street and notice that a person approaching me is holding a gun. I view the gun as dangerous, and I immediately walk, if not run in another direction. I had no available information regarding the person holding the gun. I did not take time to analyze the person who was in possession of the gun. I simply viewed the gun as dangerous, and therefore I walked away.

Example 5: *The Expedient Pathway (P→D)* provides a very simple and direct pathway to a decision. Working in a restaurant as a food server, tips are a big part of income because most employees receive minimum wages. As a restaurant server, I came to realize that some people tip more than others do. Some of my coworkers even taught me how to distinguish customers who would tip a lot from those who would not. I selected those customers who were more than likely the bigger tippers and provided them with better service.

Every time a customer walked into the restaurant, I decided whether to serve him or her. This type of thinking allowed my perception to reach a conclusion without considering "information" about the customer. The consequence was not what I had expected. Overall tips were noticeably diminished over the next few weeks. Although there were no customer complaints, my manager had noticed and given a warning. This way of process thinking allowed for no information or analysis. I made decisions to perform or not perform my duty as a server to customers based on their appearance.

The Expedient Pathway (P→D) may assume that information is not sufficient for decision-making purposes. That is, information might be filled with errors, noise, or interpretation problems. Your expertise in a particular task may serve to overcome deficient information sources. Calling on your memories, reinforced by education, training, and/or repetition of certain tasks, may aid in the resolution of a problem. Of course, the magnitude of this situation should determine if help is needed.

The $P→D$ pathway is the shortest and quickest way to come to a decision. It's known as the expedient pathway. This pathway is very concise because it only involves perception before a decision is made. It is often used when we are under severe time pressures. In addition, when the information we are given is inaccurate or unreliable, or if pieces of the information are missing, it is a very appropriate pathway depending on our expertise, as discussed in chapter 3.

If time pressures bound the situation when a decision is considered, then perceptual processing will take center function. Finally, an individual must understand or guard against the misuse of certain strategies and biases, including representativeness, availability, anchoring and adjustment, belief bias, hindsight bias, confirmation bias, conjunctive fallacy, illusory correlation, simulation strategy, familiarity, and recency effects. The $P→D$ pathway can be divided into two parts given a stable or unstable environment, which could result in different decision choices. Let's consider further examples that explore the $P→D$ pathway when the environment is stable or unstable, as presented in Figure 6.2.

Figure 6.2. P→D

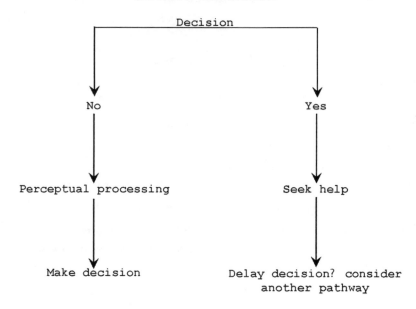

Unstable environment

Decision

No   Yes

Perceptual processing   Seek help

Make decision   Delay decision? consider
                                          another pathway

P→D (Stable Environment)

Sometimes police are faced with "shoot/no-shoot" decisions. These decisions must be made in fractions of a second and have profound consequences. A wrong decision can lead to death of a citizen. Further, exposure to environmental stressors stimulates increases in heart rate and blood pressure as well as secretion of a variety of hormones (time pressures).

Suppose a police officer is on a coffee break and has entered a convenience store to purchase a snack. It is during the early hours of the morning, and there has been no trouble in the vicinity. The convenience store is located in a pleasant neighborhood with which the police officer is familiar. After purchasing some snacks from the store, the police officer waits in line behind a man in a long coat. When the man in the coat proceeds to the front of the line, he reaches into his inside coat pocket and starts to take something out of it.

A thought passes through the police officer's head that perhaps the man with the long coat has a firearm and is planning to rob the store. However, because the police officer is familiar with the area and has been working there for some time, he is aware that the crime rate is very low (perceptual frame) and that the chances are quite low that someone would attempt this type of robbery. The police officer makes the *decision choice* not to draw his own firearm, and sure enough, the man takes out a cell phone.

P→D (Unstable Environment)

Many events in our lives are unplanned and unexpected. For example, a person is rushed to the emergency room with head injuries. After an initial assessment, patients are cared for based on the nature of the illness or injury. Those in life-threatening, critical-care situations are always given top priority. And usually this order is constantly shifting as new, unexpected patients arrive (*unstable environment*). The hospital attempts its best, under these conditions, to keep everyone apprised of an estimated time for treatment.

Suppose an emergency room doctor must decide whether or not to operate on a patient relatively soon, but she wants to consult with the resident neurologist before she makes her decision. This process illustrates how the doctor uses her perceptual frame (based on her *expertise*) to decide if the patient requires an immediate operation and how her desire for consultation contributes to a delayed action (*decision choice*) and may influence her to use another *pathway*.

Summary

The Expedient Pathway, the P→D pathway, is the most efficient decision-making pathway because it relies only on *perception* to make a decision. Perception is how we frame the environment based on our own experiences. Therefore, our emotions and personal biases can influence how a situation is framed. This pathway is characterized by a limited time period to influence a decision and the disregard of available informational sources. Many of our decisions using this pathway are based on personal expertise or a degree of experience that allows us to reinforce a strategy or bias or to draw on our own knowledge base.

CHAPTER 7

P→J→D
The Ruling Guide Pathway

Heads are wisest when they are cool and hearts are strongest when they beat in response to noble ideals.

—Ralph J. Bunche

The $P \rightarrow J \rightarrow D$ pathway implies that our framing of the problem (P) drives how and what is analyzed (J) before rendering a decision. Much of what we believe and feel can strongly influence the items or ingredients we deem important for our analysis (J). Biases and search patterns can also affect our analysis. It is important to note that this particular pathway plays down or eliminates available information sources. The reasons for overlooking information are similar to the $P \rightarrow D$ pathway. That is, time pressures, problematic information sources, unstable environmental conditions, and the degree of your experience or expertise can affect your available information use in handling a particular problem situation.

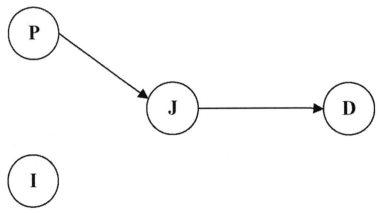

Figure 7.1. *P→J→D:* The Decision Path Is:
Perception to Judgment to Decision.

Example 1: You are standing at a street corner, after 10 PM, in a neighborhood with a very high crime rate. You approach a traffic light with the intention of crossing to the corner diagonally opposite you. You stand at the traffic light, knowing that you have to cross over to the opposite corner; therefore, it does not matter which street you cross first. Looking to your left, you notice that the other side of that street is well lit, and underneath a street lamp stands a well-dressed businesswoman carrying a briefcase.

Across the street to your right is a man dressed in old, dirty jeans, holding a broken wine bottle. The streetlight above him is broken, and there is nobody else on that side of the street to help you should the man try to hurt you. The streetlight turns green, allowing you to cross to the side where the man is standing. You deliberate which side to cross first. Then you wait, and when the other light turns green, you cross to the side with the businesswoman and go on your way.

This pathway illustrates that perception is relied on heavily en route to a decision choice. According to this pathway (*P→J→D*), there was no information on the businesswoman or the poorly-dressed man. Individuals who are not experts in the situation at hand often use this pathway. As with any other pathway relying on perception, strategies play a big part. For instance, the idea that an individual carrying a broken bottle at night is likely to commit a crime might flash through a person's mind. Hence, this type of a previous episodic memory may influence and help frame an individual's judgment.

Example 2: The P→J→D mode of decision making can vary greatly depending on the situation. Take the case of a teenager who is bitten by a big dog. After a few months have passed, she is walking down a street at night and stops at a four-stop intersection. She wants to cross the street to the opposite corner, where a large, unattended dog is standing. She can either go directly across the street or go along the perimeter of the intersection to reach her destination.

The woman is more likely to walk around the perimeter of the intersection instead of directly across it, even if it is a longer route. This is partially due to a representative strategy that she has developed in response to her prior bad experience with a big dog. In this particular example, a judgment was made in uncertainty because she just assumed that the dog across the street was bad. She was unsure; therefore she made the decision with "lower risk" involved and simply avoided the situation altogether.

Example 3: An availability strategy plays a major role in the following example. Ruth goes to Best Buy with the intent of purchasing a stereo set. She finds two stereos that she likes very much. The first one is a brand that she's never heard of, and the second one is a Sony brand. The "no-recognition" brand is at a cheaper price than the Sony, though it appears to be similar. Because she is not in a hurry, she weighs her options carefully. Ruth believes that the Sony brand is of better quality and is easier to get serviced because of the large corporate backing.

The $P→J→D$, the way known as the "ruling guide pathway," implies that the way we perceptually frame a situation determines how we analyze the problem before making a decision. In this pathway biases could play a huge role. Personal, societal, and acquired biases can change what we believe.

Specifically, as discussed in chapter 3, quite a few strategies and biases can enter into your perception. For example, some of these strategies and biases include representativeness, availability, anchoring and adjustment, belief bias, hindsight bias, confirmation bias, conjunctive fallacy, illusory correlation, simulation strategy, familiarity, and recency effects. When a person uses this pathway, either they are ignoring information or the information is not adequate to make a decision.

Expertise can guide individuals with situations that are recognizable. However, if the person isn't an expert in the field or experienced in the situation, then it can lead to detrimental decisions. The $P{\rightarrow}J{\rightarrow}D$ pathway can be divided into two parts of a stable or unstable environment. The environmental influence could influence the type of decision choice made by an individual. Let's consider further examples that explore the $P{\rightarrow}J{\rightarrow}D$ pathway when the environment is stable or unstable, as presented in Figure 7.2.

Figure 7.2. $P{\rightarrow}J{\rightarrow}D$

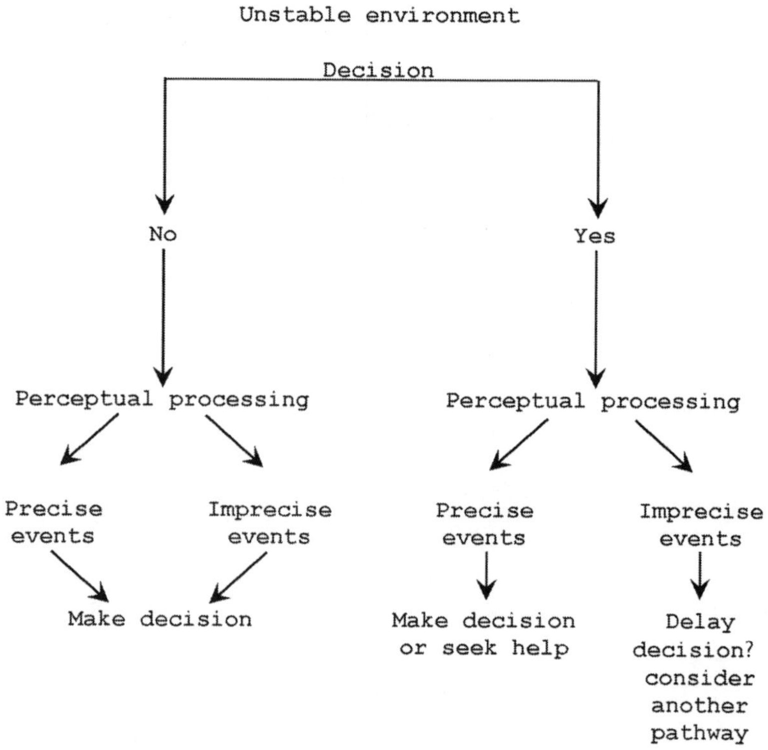

Unstable environment

Decision

No

Yes

Perceptual processing

Perceptual processing

Precise
events

Imprecise
events

Precise
events

Imprecise
events

Make decision

Make decision
or seek help

Delay
decision?
consider
another
pathway

P→J→D (Stable Environment)

Voting registration is required for the primary, general, municipal, and countywide elections. To register, one must be a U.S. citizen, 18 years old, and a bona fide state and county resident (typically a 30-day minimum residency). Most cities have city–county joint registration. You must reregister if you move, have a name change, or fail to vote at a primary or general election during a specified time period.

People can obtain mail-in registration forms in the drivers' license office, health and welfare departments, and other state agencies. Registration closes several days prior to the election. An individual decides to vote in the state election for choosing a governor, senators, and other state officials but has no idea or information on the candidates. However, she decides to vote for the Green Party candidates because she believes (*perceptual framing*) they are more concerned about environmental issues. She ranks the most desirable features of the candidates to the least desirable features based on party affiliation (*precise events*). Finally, she votes for all the Green Party candidates (*decision choice*).

Assuming that she cannot rank the most desirable features of the candidates to the least desirable features based on party affiliation (*imprecise events*), she still votes for all the Green Party candidates (*decision choice*).

P→J→D (Unstable Environment)

Robert gets off work late and has the option of either walking home or taking the bus. However, it has been raining on and off during the day, and he has not confirmed whether it will be raining when he gets off work. In other words, he has no information to help him in a changing weather environment.

Robert is very thrifty; therefore, he prefers not to ride on the bus. He knows that his walk home will be through a poorly lighted street in a neighborhood that he believes has a fair amount of crime, but he's very familiar with the area, and he is not concerned about the possibility of running into harm's way (*perceptual framing*). He ranks and compare features such as rain possibility, safeness, and pleasantness of walking home as being "moderate" (*precise events*). His analysis (*judgment*) is that it is very safe to walk home on a well-traveled pedestrian route (*decision choice*).

Let's assume that Robert has great difficulty in comparing this neighborhood to others in terms of features such as safeness and pleasantness for walking home. Given the nature of ordering these attributes (*imprecise events*), he may delay his decision if there are *no time pressures* or consider another pathway. This may result in a *decision* to ride the bus.

Summary

The Ruling Guide Pathway, $P{\rightarrow}J{\rightarrow}D$ illustrates a decision-making process from *perception* through *judgment* to *decision choice*. This pathway is characterized as a perceptual framing of the decision in which you may have biases and strategies, time pressures, a rejection of new informational sources, and a certain degree of expertise. This pathway is equally useful in handling situations from both stable and unstable environments.

CHAPTER 8

I→J→D
The Analytical Pathway

Wisdom denotes the pursuing of the best
ends by the best means.

—Frances Hutcheson

The $I{\rightarrow}J{\rightarrow}D$ pathway implies that available information sources (I) have a direct impact on our analysis (J) before a decision is made. This particular pathway appears to be more analytical than the other pathways in that perceptual framing (P) is downplayed or is not part of this decision-making course of action. The information sources (I) have been predetermined and are weighted in terms of their impact on the analysis function (J). In addition, the information sources are deemed to be reliable and programmable. Although changes in the environment may occur, the information sources (I) used by an individual typically do not change. The $I{\rightarrow}J{\rightarrow}D$ pathway works well when the environment is stable and the information sources are reliable and relevant.

Example 1: Your mother is planning on taking time off from work to go on a family vacation. To receive the time off, she is required to apply for it well in advance. She knows that the family will be leaving on June 28 and returning on July 7. With this information in hand, she judges that she will need an extra day before the departure date to pack for the trip. Thus, she decides to apply for vacation from June 27 to July 7.

Example 2: I decide to go out to eat at a fast-food restaurant for lunch. The closest fast-food restaurants near my home are McDonald's, Burger King, Wendy's, Taco Bell, Del Taco, Pizza Hut, and Domino's Pizza. Using a noncompensatory model, I proceed to eliminate alternatives. First, I desire to eat at a fast-food restaurant with an "A" grade from the Los Angeles County Health Department. Burger King has a "B" grade; hence I eliminate it as a choice. Next, I am not in the mood to eat pizza; therefore, I quickly remove Pizza Hut and Domino's as possible places to eat. Further, I just ate at Taco Bell and Del Taco a few days ago, and I usually do not want to repeat eating at the same restaurant in a week. Therefore, I eliminate Taco Bell and Del Taco. I am left with McDonald's and Wendy's. From this point on, I switch to a compensatory model. I assign points to the dimensions of reliability, variety, and overall taste. McDonald's receives a score of 5 for reliability, 5 for variety, and 3 for overall taste. Wendy's receives a score of 4 for reliability, 4 for variety, and 3 for overall taste. Hence, McDonald's receives the highest overall score with 13, so I eat at McDonald's.

Example 3: I arrive at a cellular telephone store to purchase a cell phone. I immediately notice that there are three major carriers for cellular phones: Super Wireless, Excellent Cellular, and Best Phones. Super Wireless is the most reliable but also the most expensive service. Excellent Cellular offers decent plans at decent prices. Best Phones offers great plans with only moderate coverage. The pertinent information I have is that I need at least 1,500 minutes per month, and that I am hoping not to spend more than $50 per month. I also know that I need long distance built into my plan because I am going out of state for college. After assigning weights to these three plans, I finally notice that Super Wireless scored quite high on the dominant criteria for the cellular phone selection. That is, Super Wireless rated higher on the dominant criteria than the other carriers. Feeling confident about my selection, I sign up with Super Wireless.

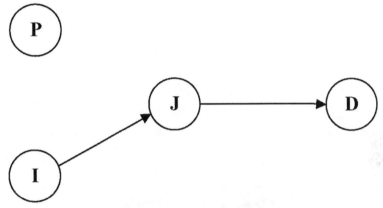

Figure 8.1. *I→J→D* Decision Path:
Information to Judgment to Decision.

The *I→J→D* pathway is known as the analytical pathway. This pathway removes any form of perception and relies heavily on the information that is available. However, relying solely on information sources can cause problems if the information is incomplete, noisy, and/or difficult to interpret. This pathway works best when the environment is stable and the information is reliable and relevant. The *I→J→D* pathway can be divided into two parts given a stable or unstable environment, which could result in different decision choices. Let's consider further examples that explore the *I→J→D* pathway when the environment is stable or unstable, as presented in Figure 8.2.

Figure 8.2. I→J→D

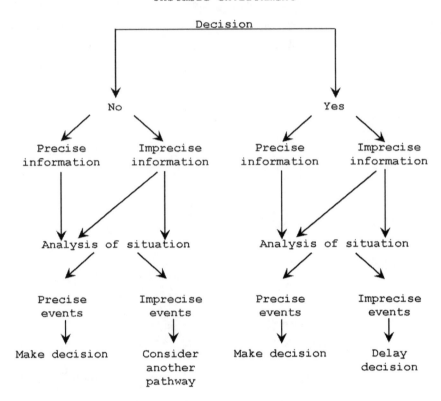

I→J→D (Stable Environment)

Learning photography underscores technical basics about camera operation, film, filters, shutter speed/aperture values, and other mechanical details. You are shown good-looking pictures, some with technical shooting data, illustrating concepts like "depth of field" and "slow shutter speed photography," zoom lenses, lighting, and what a flash will do. Let's say that you are in a beginning photography class, and your assignment is to take abstract pictures of objects or images and make prints. Your instructor points outs that you can be very creative in taking your pictures. You were taught in class that abstract photos can be images of normal objects that are seen from a different point of view than the way they are typically viewed. You decide to go out to take pictures on a sunny afternoon.

The next day is Saturday, and you have plenty of time to search for abstract objects. Because it is a sunny day, you can take advantage of a stable environment, in that you have plenty of light for your pictures. You find out from watching a weather report that there will be clear, blue skies all day Saturday. Consequently you do not have to worry about grainy prints from low lighting as long as you find objects that are outside and have light. You have *precise information* for working on your project, in that you know you need to create an abstract print. You have all the information you need to complete your assignment, in that you know how to operate your single-lens reflex camera, you know that the weather will be sunny all day Saturday, and you know that you can compare different photographic objects.

Therefore, you analyze (*judgment*) and arrange learned information, such as f-stop aperture and shutter speed, to create a quality photograph (*precise events*). Based on these ideal conditions, you decide (*decision choice*) to go out and take pictures.

Suppose you missed attending several class meetings, and your understanding of technical basics about camera operation, film, filters, shutter speed/aperture values, and other mechanical details is incomplete (*imprecise information*). You may still complete the assignment if other information learned in class can assist you in your analysis (*judgment*) and arrangement of key information, such as f-stop aperture and shutter speed, to create a quality photograph (*precise events*). However, if the *imprecise information* is difficult to analyze, resulting in *imprecise events*, then it would be better to seek another pathway for making a decision to take the pictures.

I→J→D (Unstable Environment)

William is a technician who works for a police Explosive Ordnance Disposal unit, sometimes referred to as the Bomb Squad. Bomb technicians are responsible for the secure removal, transport, and storage of explosives. They perform bomb scene investigations, collect and protect evidence, provide technical support for special operations, and amass and convey technical information on explosive devices and incidents. William's supervisor informs him that there is a bomb at a nearby shopping mall and tells him to take care of the situation immediately.

The only information William has is from his supervisor, who he believes is very reliable. William understands that he has to go to the shopping mall and defuse the bomb. He analyzes the situation at the shopping mall, given the supervisor's information (*precise information*), and he is able to determine which of the wires should be cut first based on its colors (*precise events*). Finally, William defuses the bomb (*make decision*).

Assume that the supervisor's information is incomplete due to time pressures or changing conditions regarding knowledge about the bomb. Because of William's many years of bomb experience, he is able to determine which of the wires should be cut first with its colors (*precise events*). This analysis results in William defusing the bomb. However, if the ordering of the colored wires is confusing (*imprecise events*), then William's *decision choice* would be a delayed decision until further orders from his supervisor to take further action.

Summary

The analytical pathway, $I{\rightarrow}J{\rightarrow}D$, consists of achieving the most usefulness from your decision given reliable and relevant information. On the other hand, information that is incomplete, noisy, and/or difficult to interpret weakens the interpretation of this pathway. This pathway assumes that all information is known, the environment is controllable, and the information is precise, in that it can be compared to other events or that it can be rated or ranked. Typically, the environment is stable, and the information and events are precise.

CHAPTER 9

I→P→D
The Revisionist Pathway

A prudent person profits from personal experience, a wise one from the experience of others.

—Joseph Collins

The $I{\rightarrow}P{\rightarrow}D$ pathway implies that available information sources (I) can influence our framing (P) of the problem before arriving at a decision (D). In this pathway, available information sets the stage as it informs or alters our perception (P) en route to a decision. Information is deemed very important and not to be ignored, thereby providing updates to our memories. Our updated memories are used to bypass a more detailed analysis (J) due to time pressures, experience, or an unstable environment.

Information serves as the starting point in terms of providing the necessary signals to help shape our view of the situation before any action is taken. Note that the Expedient Pathway ($P{\rightarrow}D$) serves as a subset to the Revisionist Pathway. That is to say that information is effectively used even though there may be a degree of incompleteness, noise interference, and interpretational problems.

However, these degrees of difficulty are not enough to downplay or ignore the information sources (*I*). As with the Expedient Pathway, time pressures may be sufficiently high to warrant bypassing a more detailed analysis (*J*) in a *decision choice*. Further, the instability of the environment may also contribute to the fact that the *judgment* (analysis) process (*J*) is not too useful.

The *I*→*P*→*D* pathway may also indicate that people may make decisions based on information they are given, whether it is accurate or not. If the information conforms to what they have already perceived, they may make a decision based on it. For instance, most individuals who are part of a university setting believe that a postsecondary education is very important in a competitive nation like the United States.

When students are asked why they decided to pursue a postsecondary education, they respond that it prepares them for the workforce and that they will make more money than people who do not go to a university (*P*).

Further, information provided by a business magazine states that college graduates are highly respected, and their income per year is twice that of those who do not complete a postsecondary education. They are given jobs and promotions at a faster rate than those who drop out without education. Their beginning salary is usually higher than past employees. Based on this information, a high school student who reads the business magazine and already has a similar perception that he or she will be more independent and financially stable after graduation from college will then decide to go to college (*D*).

Example 1: When you are considering purchasing a personal computer, the store employees may provide you with product information. This information, however, may be biased toward products with a higher markup that will enable the store to become more profitable. Most likely, you will weight their selected information more heavily. Why? The salesperson providing the information may have more knowledge about the personal computers than you.

Example 2: The $I{\rightarrow}P{\rightarrow}D$ pathway looms large for people who tune into a television home shopping network and have an urge to buy whatever is being sold if they think it's a good price, regardless of the product value. They are only given price information, and they believe it to be a bargain. Therefore, they buy the product without considering its usefulness.

Example 3: Eighth grade ends in a few months, and high school approaches very soon. I live in Love-it-City, and three high schools are close to my residence. My parents and I researched the three schools and obtained some information. Love-it-City High School, the school I would attend, has always possessed a good academic reputation and a better reputation than the two other schools.

More students enter universities from Love-it-City High School than from the other two schools. Love-it-City High School's students also score higher on the SAT and have higher GPAs. In terms of location, the school is next to the city library and the police department. Based on these facts, my parents and I perceive the school as very safe, convenient, and academically sound. However, we have completely neglected to consider other factors and negatives while falling under the so-called confirmation trap. We considered information that helped shape or form our perception and failed to consider the defects of Love-it-City High School and attributes of the other schools (that is, no detailed analysis or judgment).

We also used the belief that crime around Love-it-City High School is lessened due to the close proximity of the police department and the routine presence of police officers in the area. We failed to realize that incidences of crime can still occur on campus and after school at Love-it-

City High School and that academic reputation can change over time. My family and I lacked the expertise regarding the ranking and selection of high schools.

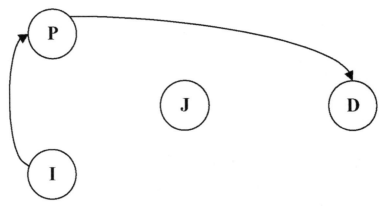

Figure 9.1. *I→P→D*: The Process Thinking Goes from Information to Perception and to Decision.

The *I→P→D* pathway is known as the "revisionist pathway" because information can influence or revise a person's perceptions. The information in this situation must be used efficiently to maximize the function of the pathway. When using this pathway, the person must believe that information is reliable and accurate. That is, information that is incomplete, noisy, and/or difficult to interpret can bias a decision. Time pressures or an unstable environment can force a person to use this pathway because they may not have time to analyze the situation. The *I→P→D* pathway can be divided into two parts given a stable or unstable environment, which could result in different decision choices. Let's consider further examples that explore the *I→P→D* pathway when the environment is stable or unstable, as presented in Figure 9.2.

Figure 9.2. I→P→D

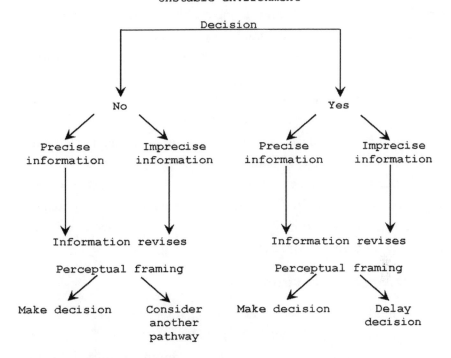

I→P→D (Stable Environment)

Suppose you go to a jewelry store to purchase a diamond ring for your spouse. Understanding the *cut, clarity, color,* and *carat weight* of a diamond is essential to getting the best quality diamond for the best price. You are given the following information (*precise information*) from the salesperson

A well-cut diamond is symmetrically round with a proper depth and width. It reflects light like a mirror from one facet to another and disperses and reflects this light through the top of the stone. Clarity in diamonds measures the effect of inclusions, such as fractures, scratches, or trace minerals. Perfectly clear diamonds are referred to as flawless and rare.

Diamonds are like prisms because they can partition light into a spectrum of colors and reflect this light in colorful flashes referred to as *fire*. The more colorless a diamond is, the more colorful the fire will appear. One carat is equivalent to 200 milligrams. At times, one carat is referred to as 100 points. A measurement of 0.5 carat would then be the same as 50 points, or a half carat. Because larger diamonds are not as common as smaller diamonds, the cost increases exponentially with an increase in weight.

The preceding information influences your personal preferences (*perceptual framing*) before you make a decision to buy.

Assume that you walk into a large discount department store, and a salesperson does not give you details regarding a diamond's *cut, clarity, color,* and *carat weight* (*imprecise information*). The influence on your perceptual framing may not be sufficient to enable you to purchase a diamond ring wisely. In this type of situation, you may want to consider a different decision-making pathway.

I→P→D (Unstable Environment)

Decision makers must often formulate decisions in unstable environments. During the late-1970s, Schwinn Bicycle Company was slow to respond to the advent of the mountain bicycle (*precise information*). Unfortunately, management believed (*perceptual framing*) that the surge in mountain bicycles was just another fad. Schwinn's reluctance to make a *decision choice* to introduce a mountain bicycle cost the company its dominance in the American bicycle market and contributed to its eventual bankruptcy.

A manufacturer must decide at times whether or not to embrace a new technology in a changing environment. During the late 1980s, Xerox gathered pieces of information that reported on Japanese semiconductor manufacturers shifting resources to a new, X-ray-based manufacturing method (*imprecise information*). Xerox believed (*perceptual framing*) that this was the way to go and made a decision choice to reallocate significant company resources to this new approach. Years later, it was quite evident that such a shift did not occur and, in fact, would not occur in the foreseeable future. Perhaps it would have been more appropriate for Xerox to *delay* its decision. The difficulty of separating good information signals from noisy or incorrect information can lead to overreaction in decision making.

Summary

The Revisionist Pathway, $I{\rightarrow}P{\rightarrow}D$, applies the use of information that influences perception and allows for a decision to be made. Characteristics of this pathway include available information that can aid in framing the environment. This pathway differs from the $P{\rightarrow}D$ pathway in that information is not ignored, but rather emphasized during the decision-making process. Information plays a part in revising perception as well, thereby influencing individuals' strategies and biases.

There can be an unstable environment, and there may be a lack of expertise because perception may be strongly influenced by the information. A drawback to this pathway is that individuals may use information that is incomplete, noisy, and/or difficult to interpret in their decision-making process. Finally, there is no judgment function to analyze or check processed information before rendering a decision. Of course, if time pressures are great, then this pathway may be appropriate given that the decision must be made quickly.

CHAPTER 10

P→I→J→D
The Value-Driven Pathway

If virtue promises happiness, prosperity
and peace, then progress in virtue is
progress in each of these; for to whatever
point the perfection of anything brings us,
progress is always an approach toward it.

—Epictetus

The *P→I→J→D* pathway asserts that perception (*P*) shapes and guides
the various types of information sources (*I*) that will be used in our analysis
(*J*) during a decision choice (*D*). Our framing of a particular problem
suggests the various types of information sources that will selected and
weighted for further analysis (*J*) to make a decision (*D*).

Undoubtedly, perceptual framing (*P*) provides the conveyor belt of
influencing any or all types of information that will be selected, weighted,
and used in the analysis process (*J*). This conveyor belt helps our social
conditioning in various knowledge forms. These knowledge forms provide
meanings and definitions to people, places, and things. Therefore, our
handling of a situation is strongly influenced by our education, training,

social, and economic perspective. These perspectives help to ferret out the information sources that will be implemented for further analysis (*J*).

Yet another aspect of the Value-Driven Pathway is that it embodies the Analytical Pathway (*I*→*J*→*D*). Or another way of describing this embodiment is to view the perceptual frame (*P*) as a conditioning influence on an analytical and programmatic way of reaching a decision. The highlight of the Value-Driven Pathway is that it can modify or discard informational sources used in analysis (*J*).

Recall from chapter 2 that the Analytical Pathway represents an analytical and programmatic approach, which includes specifying the problem, identifying all factors, weighting factors, identifying all alternatives, rating alternatives on each factor, and choosing the optimal alternative. Well, the Value-Driven Pathway can change the factors, weights, and alternatives used in the analysis function. The perceptual frame brings about this change!

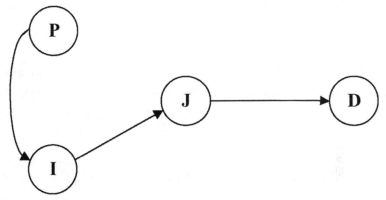

Figure 10.1. *P*→*I*→*J*→*D*:
Perception to Information to Judgment to Decision.

Example 1: I was searching for a job during the summer. I wasn't sure exactly what I wanted to do for the summer; however, I knew I wanted a job. Therefore, I started to look around, browsing want ads on the Internet and in newspapers and observing workers at various businesses, to determine which ones interested me the most. I thought, from what I had perceived, that working in retail wasn't a bad job, and it had relatively flexible hours. I also knew that I wanted to work in an electronics or computer store, and not in a store that sold clothing or other types of goods. I began to compile a mental list of the jobs that interested me, and then I went about my research.

I started talking to different managers at a variety of stores to gain a better sense of what the salaries and responsibilities were for positions I was interested in applying for. I also learned how flexible a particular manager was at a certain company, and I eventually walked away with a good idea of what job I really wanted. I made this determination through my judgment, which was based on my initial perception and the information I had gathered. A few months later I went to work for CompUSA, the company I wanted to work for.

Because I had started with perception, this particular pathway was subject to strategies and biases, such that I preferred to work in a computer store rather than an electronics store such as The Good Guys. This already slanted my perception and initial evaluation of the jobs that were available, and then the information confirmed that particular notion when I discovered that the job at CompUSA seemed to be a much more relaxed. I didn't want to bore or exhaust myself the summer before college. Hence my initial perception and information matched, and I decided to select CompUSA.

Example 2: It is very late one Wednesday night. I check the time on my wristwatch and see that it is almost 1:00 AM! I do not want to sleep yet because my computer has 15 minutes to go in downloading a movie, but I have a class to attend in 7 hours. I need some rest for my morning class, or else fatigue will cause me to be sleepy during class. I began downloading the movie around midnight. Should I cancel the download and go to sleep, losing an hour for nothing, or continue downloading and lose fifteen minutes of precious sleep?

My sleep should take priority, but commitment tells me to continue downloading because I've already used an hour of my time. I convince myself that I can lose 15 minutes of sleep rather than an hour of downloading a movie. Further, due to technical problems, I cannot go to sleep and let the downloading continue. Finishing the download is more important to me than sleeping. Hence, I delay my sleep by 15 minutes.

Example 3: I knew I had to apply to colleges during my senior year of high school; therefore, I started to compile a list of the colleges I wanted to possibly attend. I first used my perception, to categorize and classify colleges I thought would make a good match for me, and then I made a preliminary list. After the list was compiled, I started to use available information to research the colleges. I visited them, acquired literature on them, and talked with admission representatives. Next, I took my initial list and referenced the colleges with my information, ranking and rating ones to keep in my analysis (J), before arriving at a final decision (D).

The $P{\rightarrow}I{\rightarrow}J{\rightarrow}D$ pathway is known as the "value-driven pathway" because our perceptions change or how we interpret the information that is available to us changes. The information will also be weighted based on how we have framed the situation.

However, extra care must be taken to acknowledge that certain strategies or biases may be a part of our perceptions, thereby affecting the available information set. For example, some of these include representativeness, availability, anchoring and adjustment, belief bias, hindsight bias, confirmation bias, conjunctive fallacy, illusory correlation, simulation strategy, and familiarity and recency effects. This is a good pathway to use when the person is an expert on the situation, isn't under time pressures, and has reliable information.

The $P{\rightarrow}I{\rightarrow}J{\rightarrow}D$ pathway can be divided into two parts, given a stable or unstable environment, which could result in different decision choices. Let's consider further examples that explore the $P{\rightarrow}I{\rightarrow}J{\rightarrow}D$ pathway when the environment is either stable or unstable, as presented in Figure 10.2.

Figure 10.2. P→I→J→D

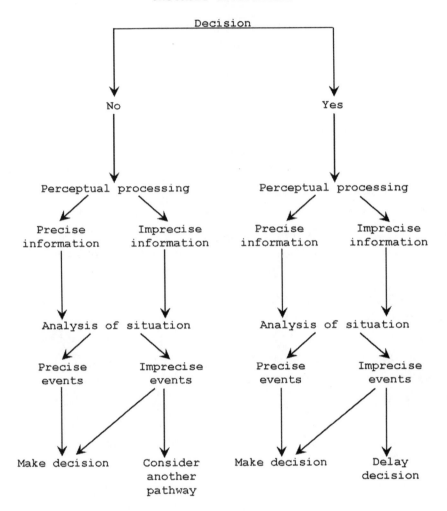

P→I→J→D (Stable Environment)

After viewing many commercials regarding the military, a young woman believes she should join the Air Force (*perception*). She loves playing *Star Wars* video games and enjoys bungee jumping. She finds out that there are over 4,100 different officer and enlisted jobs offered by the military. She takes a military test to learn more about her interests, as well as to identify and explore potentially satisfying occupations and develop an effective strategy to realize her goal (*precise information*). These results are integrated with her personal preferences to help her identify and prioritize possible career choices (*precise events*). This process results in a decision to join or not to join the Air Force that can benefit her throughout her work life.

Assume that the military commercials have only provided the woman with information on how service in the armed forces can provide money for her college education (*imprecise information*). Further, she has watched many documentaries and war movies to somewhat comprehend the grisly realities of combat. When analyzing this information along with her personal feelings (*perception*), she finds it very difficult to determine whether becoming a good military officer would outweigh the fear of tragedy in the military or vice versa (*imprecise events*). Therefore, she could make a decision whether to join or use one of the other dominant pathways to assist her in decision making.

P→I→J→D (Unstable Environment)

Automobiles are the second-largest expense we have in our lives after our homes. Assume you are planning to purchase a used automobile in the next month; however, you are uncertain about whether you will be laid off from your job. The additional expense, if you are without a job, could cause you serious financial problems. Therefore, your perception sways the information that you obtain before your decision analysis.

If you are dealing with precise information regarding your future with the company, this could help assist your analysis to purchase a used automobile. That is, information regarding arranging financing for the automobile purchase and the monthly payments can be estimated based on the price, selection, and reliability of the used car. Also, to avoid future repair expenses, you could have the automobile inspected by a diagnostic mechanic to see whether it has been wrecked or has any major defects.

You also check with *Consumer Reports'* listings of car models that have performed well. You check the used car price for reasonability with, let's say, Edmund's or Kelly Blue Book Web site. Finally, for the vehicle you want to purchase, you pay a nominal fee for a history report from carfax.com. You can now analyze (*judgment*) the information and compare different used cars with one another (*precise events*), and then you can make a decision to buy or not to buy a used car.

Assume that the information is fragmented (*imprecise information*), and it is difficult to determine information regarding arranging financing for the automobile purchase as well as estimating monthly payments. You can affectively order the probability of being out of work for one or two months (*precise events*) and calculate your income over that period to pay for your purchased automobile. Then make a decision to buy or not buy the used car.

If the information is fragmented (*imprecise information*) and you can affectively order the probability of being out of work for one or two months, (*imprecise events*), then you should delay the decision.

Summary

Pathway $P \rightarrow I \rightarrow J \rightarrow D$, known as the Value-Driven Pathway, consists of perception manipulating the information set, which in turn influences judgment on a decision. Because perception influences information, the information can be modified. Also, it is possible that biases and strategies may be more heavily weighted in regard to people, places, and things. This pathway allows individuals to make changes in their decision-making process as well as rating, ranking, and sorting their judgments before making a decision choice. In addition, decision making on this pathway can be determined through our experiences from political, economic, management, financial, and social elements.

CHAPTER 11

I→P→J→D
The Global Perspective Pathway

I do the very best I know how—the very
best I can; and mean to keep doing so until
the end. If the end brings me out all right,
what is said against me won't amount to
anything. If the end brings me out wrong,
ten angels swearing I was right would make
no difference.

—Abraham Lincoln

The *I→P→J→D* pathway indicates that information sources (*I*) are enabling us to update or modify our perception (*P*) before analysis (*J*) begins during a decision choice (*D*). Therefore, an open-minded viewpoint of an individual is possible when considering the various types of information sources that will indelibly influence perceptions. Our new informed perceptions will help guide the analysis (*J*) to be undertaken before reaching a decision.

Because this pathway starts with information having an influential impact on perception, it allows an individual to focus on a variety of informational sources. In chapter 2, information was viewed as *conditioned* data that has properties of relevance and reliability. That is, relevant information relates to past, present, and/or future events, whereas reliability is associated with correctness, reproduction, and confirmation of information sources.

The challenge for individuals' perceptual framing (P) is to devise a system to process information (I). This process takes on the following dimensions: (1) recognizing the usefulness of information, and identifying biases and errors in it; (2) establishing a system that alerts for changing information; and (3) providing a system that matches incoming information with our framing of it. Therefore, this pathway is duly referred to as the Global Perspective Pathway because most incoming information sources are deemed possible for further processing by perceptual framing (P) and analysis (J).

However, this perspective can be immensely weakened by time pressure situations. That is, time pressure situations can cause an individual to hurry the decision-making process due to a lack of time to consider all relevant sources of information. Further, unstable environments bringing about sudden shifts in the interpretation of information sources can also present problems with this particular pathway.

Interestingly enough, the Ruling Guide Pathway ($P{\rightarrow}J{\rightarrow}D$) can be viewed as a subset of the Global Perspective Pathway ($I{\rightarrow}P{\rightarrow}J{\rightarrow}D$). Apparently, decision rules ($P{\rightarrow}J{\rightarrow}D$) are utilized after incoming information sources are considered to modify the Ruling Guide Pathway. The power of the Global Perspective Pathway lies in its discernment of all types of information sources.

Typically, the $I{\rightarrow}P{\rightarrow}J{\rightarrow}D$ pathway is independent of time pressures because time is used to gather information and form a judgment by assessing the situation before making the decision. Uncertainty can lie in two aspects of this pathway. First, it can be part of the reliability of the information. Second, it can be part of the perception of framing the situation. When all aspects of this pathway are controlled, however, there is a better chance of a good decision being made.

The *information* gathered must be reliable, especially if it comes from a variety of sources. *Perception* enters the process when we make decisions about the relevance of the information for further processing. *Judgment* and *decision choice* are strongly influenced by our perception of the situation and the relevance and reliability of the information in most situations.

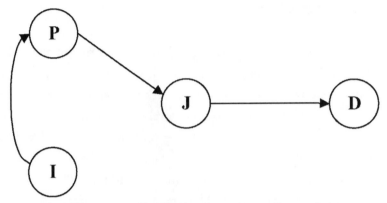

Figure 11.1. $I{\rightarrow}P{\rightarrow}J{\rightarrow}D$: Information to Perception to
Judgment to Decision.

Example 1: A particular chemistry laboratory experiment involving paper chromatography serves as a good illustration of the $I{\rightarrow}P{\rightarrow}J{\rightarrow}D$ pathway. A diluted solution of sodium hydroxide, or lye, (NaOH) is placed on a piece of chromatography paper, and the paper indicates that the pH of the solution is 13 on a scale of 1–14; with 1 being extremely acidic, 7 being neutral, and 14 being extremely basic. The pH of 13 would lead to the conclusion that NaOH is a base. The information in this experiment was furnished by the paper chromatography. The framing of the situation (P), influenced by the information, guided the process of the result (J). The reasoning processes underlying this decision-making pathway lead to the decision that the material is a base.

Example 2: When our family was looking for a new house, we had a list of several houses for sale, along with their features (that is, bedrooms, bathrooms, living area, and more) as well as their prices. This information served as our starting point, whereby we eliminated many of the houses based on their features. We then went to view the houses, which comprised the *perception* part of this pathway. Combining the information sources along with our perception, bounded by how much we could afford to spend, we were able to rank the homes. We decided to select the house that we ranked the highest.

Example 3: When I was negotiating for my salary at my job with Circuit City, I began with some basic information. This available information came from my friends pertaining to people who work in retail and how much they were paid per hour. Also, I read about the level of responsibility for the job I was applying for at Circuit City. My perceptual frame modified these information sources when I met the general manager to discuss employment. The manager seemed quite open and receptive toward me, so I decided to ask for what I wanted—$9.00 an hour. He agreed with my offer.

In this situation, the information was the starting point for the salary that I requested. If I did not have any relevant information, I may have asked for an outrageous amount or for a very small hourly rate. My perception played an instrumental role by enabling me to determine how receptive the manager was to having me as a future employee. That is, my perceptual frame influenced me to give more weight to the hourly amount that I had originally requested.

The $I{\rightarrow}P{\rightarrow}J{\rightarrow}D$ pathway is known as the Global Perspective Pathway. This pathway permits information to change our perception before analyzing and making a final decision. This pathway can weaken a decision if there are time pressures because a person may rush into making a decision, ignoring the available information sources and placing an undue amount of weight on their perceptions. An unstable environment can also change the way the information, good or bad, is interpreted, and a rushed decision is often made.

However, if unreliable information and time pressures do not limit this pathway, then there is a high probability of the best decision being made.

The $I{\rightarrow}P{\rightarrow}J{\rightarrow}D$ pathway can be divided into two parts given a stable or unstable environment, which could result in different decision choices. Let's consider further examples that explore the $I{\rightarrow}P{\rightarrow}J{\rightarrow}D$ pathway when the environment is either stable or unstable, as presented in Figure 11.2.

Figure 11.2. I→P→J→D

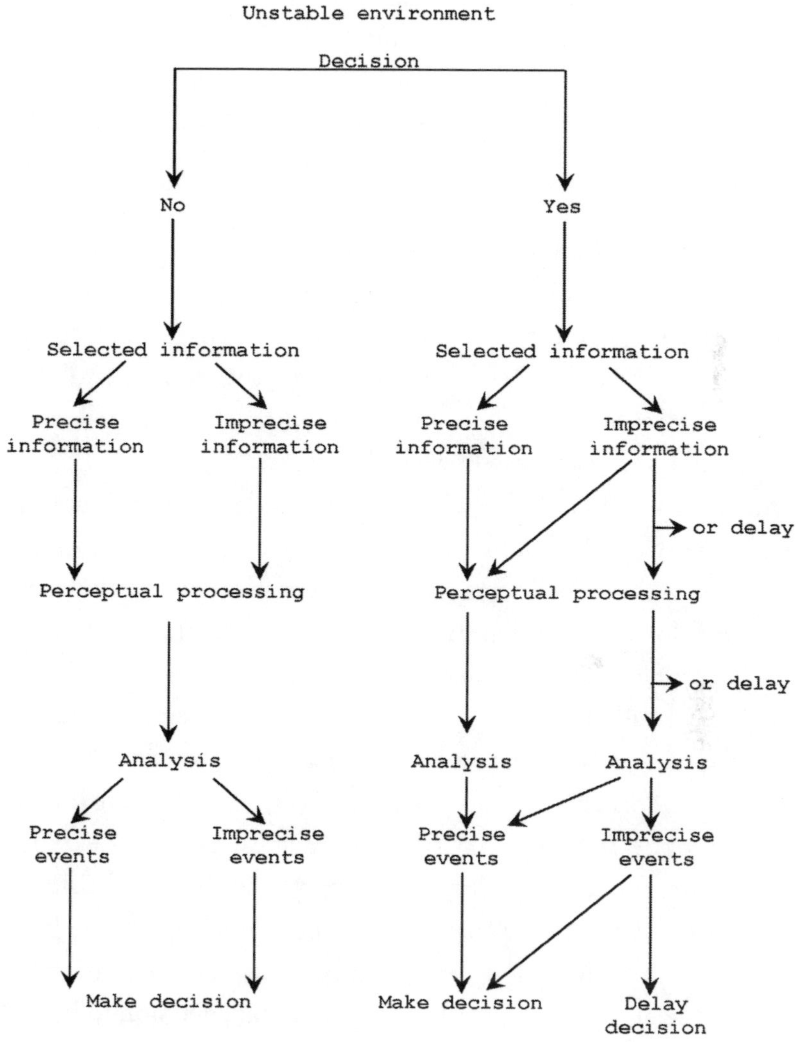

Unstable environment

I→P→J→D (Stable Environment)

An Example: Joanna decides she would like to have plastic surgery on her nose, and there is no foreseeable major event to cause future instability (for example, loss of job, money). She knows very little about plastic surgery. Therefore, she researches what a nose job would entail. From her research, she finds that plastic surgery on the nose, also known as rhinoplasty, is one of the most common cosmetic surgery procedures performed by plastic surgeons. She also discovers that rhinoplasty can reduce or increase the size of her nose, change the shape of her nose, or change the angle between her nose and her upper lip. She also learns that she is a good candidate for rhinoplasty in that she is looking for improvement, not perfection, in the way she looks.

Joanna finds information on the average price in her area, what the actual procedure is, and the recovery time. Joanna decides to have rhinoplasty performed on her nose; therefore, she searches for three doctors in her area. Supplied with information, she is able to tell each of the three doctors she visits exactly what she wants.

The first doctor is an old man with a lot of experience with rhinoplasty; however, he doesn't make Joanna feel comfortable. The second doctor she consulted is a young new doctor with some experience, but he becomes flirtatious with Joanna, and that makes her uncomfortable with him. The last doctor Joanna visits is a middle-aged man with a large book of photographs of all his rhinoplasty jobs. He's friendly and very knowledgeable about what Joanna wants to have performed on her nose.

Hence, in this process, Joanna researched what exactly is required in rhinoplasty (*precise information*). This information shapes the type of doctor she desires to have to perform the surgery, and the initial visits with the doctors created the perceptual frame in her mind (*P*). Next, Joanna analyzes the information along with her perceptions to assist her in ranking the surgeons (*precise events*), leading to a final decision to have the third doctor perform the surgery (*D*).

Assume that Joanna lives in a small town with only two plastic surgeons in a 300-mile radius, and both have just begun their practices. She would have very limited information on the surgeons (*imprecise information*). However, she could continue perceptual framing if she desires, even though the information is not complete. Her analysis would continue, although she would not be able to determine through comparison which would be the best plastic surgeon for her (*imprecise events*) when making her choice.

I→P→J→D (Unstable Environment)

An Example: Oscar has been given insider information about his friend's company's stock during a period of economic instability in the marketplace. *Insider trading* is an expression that many investors have heard, and more often than not they associate it with illegal conduct. Nevertheless, the term actually includes both legal and illegal conduct. The legal version is when corporate insiders such as officers, directors, and employees buy and sell securities in their own companies. When corporate insiders trade in their own securities, they must report their trades to the Securities and Exchange Commission. Illegal insider trading suggests buying or selling a security in breach of a fiduciary duty or other relationship of trust and confidence while in possession of material, nonpublic information about the security. Insider trading infringements include "tipping" such information, securities trading by the person "tipped," and securities trading by those who misappropriate such information.

Oscar knows that insider trading is illegal and that he should pretend he was never tipped about this information. However, Oscar is in financial hard times and could use the extra money if he follows the insider information. Oscar takes the information (*precise information*) he has been given, which, in turn, influences his perception of the consequences of insider trading, analyzes (*precise events*) what could happen to him if he gets caught, and finally decides not to partake in insider trading due to its unethical nature. This is a very unstable environment because the stock market can fluctuate to extremes on a daily basis, and Oscar cannot be sure what will happen to him as a result of the insider trading information given to him.

Assume Oscar is faced with fragmented information (*precise information*) as to whether insider trading is legal or illegal. He can *delay* his decision until he receives better information. Hence, his decision making ends at this point. However, if he continues to process the fragmented information, allowing it to influence his perception regarding his dire financial condition, he has two options.

The first option is to continue to the analysis function (*judgment*), and the second option is to quit or delay processing. If he continues to the judgment function, the analysis of deciding whether or not to borrow money to invest in the stock takes two forms. First, if he can compare this investment with his other investments (*precise events*), he will make a decision to buy or not to buy. Of course, a decision to buy could lead him into big trouble with the law. That is, ignorance regarding the law is not a sufficient alibi for committing an illegal act. If he cannot compare investment choices (*imprecise events*), he will delay his decision.

Summary

The $I{\rightarrow}P{\rightarrow}J{\rightarrow}D$ decision pathway is known as the Global Perspective Pathway because it takes into consideration all types of information sources. This pathway calls for an open-minded approach in which all possible information sources will be considered that can help update and revise the decision maker's perceptual frame. This process starts with *information* revising *perception*, followed by *judgment* to the *decision choice*. This pathway is most ideal when there are no time pressures that will limit the time it takes to compile the information and analyze the problem.

CHAPTER 12

Toward Successful Decisions with Process Thinking

> Happiness and misery depend not upon
> how high up or low down you are—they
> depend not upon these, but on the direction
> in which you are tending.
>
> —Samuel Butler

The quality of our lives can be greatly enhanced by selecting the most appropriate pathway to a decision, given a particular situation or circumstances. Although our lives are full of daily decisions, both small and large, we typically are not educated to understand which pathway can lead us to an overall superior decision! *Process thinking* helps to know when to use different combinations of perception, information, and judgment when arriving at a particular decision choice. No longer must we be confused or inundated with information inappropriate for solving a specific problem. Process thinking assists us in the careful selection of one of the six dominant pathways that can provide us with more confidence in making decisions throughout our life journey.

The decision-making pathways we take in life inspire our awareness and handling of situations. These pathways can enable us to view lovely flowers in the garden or focus more readily on the garbage flowing into the sewage drain. Our perception of our environment is not just about the information we receive, but how this information is augmented, processed, and used, if at all. Our life journey may be more pleasurable if we understand that various pathways can be taken to reach a destination.

Process thinking highlights six dominant pathways for successful decision making. Process thinking alerts us to conditions such as unstable environments, time pressures, lack of expertise, and incomplete information that can greatly influence the appropriate pathway to use in a given situation.

The Expedient Pathway ($P{\rightarrow}D$) is generally used in situations where a decision must be made rapidly. In this type of scenario, an individual begins with perceptual framing of the situation before making a decision. Perception is the framing of the environment based on an individual's own experiences. Therefore, an individual's emotions, strategies, and biases can influence how a situation is framed. In addition, expertise is helpful for this particular pathway in that it assists an individual to make more consistent and appropriate decisions when there are time pressures and incomplete information sources. This pathway emphasizes the manner by which an individual perceives the situation, whereby information is either downplayed or ignored for a variety of reasons.

The Ruling Guide Pathway ($P{\rightarrow}J{\rightarrow}D$), may be used when time pressures important but are not as immediate as the $P{\rightarrow}D$ pathway. For the $P{\rightarrow}J{\rightarrow}D$ pathway, an individual frames the problem, analyzes it, and then renders a decision. An individual framing can be influenced by strategies and biases that can influence how the analysis function is conducted. That is, what an individual believes can and will affect what he or she views as pertinent and dependable, thereby strongly influencing the type of decision made. Because information is played down or ignored, it becomes very important in guarding your perception against biases. Experience or expertise is one way of assisting this type of process.

The Analytical Pathway $(I \rightarrow J \rightarrow D)$, is useful when relevant and reliable information is the hallmark of good decisions. When using this pathway, information will directly influence the judgment function before a decision is made. Ideally, the information is predetermined and is weighted by other sources, without biases. In addition, the higher the reliability and relevance of information sources, the more appropriate use of this pathway for guiding your rating and/or ranking of alternative courses of action. This pathway works the best when the environment is more stable and information is complete, has noise no interference, and/or has no interpretation problems.

The Revisionist Pathway $(I \rightarrow P \rightarrow D)$ may be used when information can influence the manner in which an individual frames the problem or situation before coming to a final decision. The information influences the perceptual frame immensely while one is driving for a decision. In addition, information is considered an important piece of this decision-making process. Information is implemented even though it might be incomplete, noisy, and/or difficult to interpret. However, one must be careful when information is imprecise (that is, incomplete, noisy, or difficult to interpret) because the decision choice is driven by the available information sources. This pathway is a convenient way of making a decision when time pressures are an issue because there is no detailed analysis involved (no judgment function).

The Value-Driven Pathway $(P \rightarrow I \rightarrow J \rightarrow D)$ can be implemented when perceptual framing influences information sources that in turns affects judgment before a decision is made. The perceptual frame can change the information sources used to be analyzed in the judgment function. Further, an individual's education and training and his or her economic and social perspectives have a major influence on how a situation is handled. This pathway can weaken a decision if there are time pressures, because an individual may hurry into making a decision, ignore the available information sources, and try to place an undue amount of weight on their perceptions.

The Global Perspective Pathway ($I{\rightarrow}P{\rightarrow}J{\rightarrow}D$) determines how information helps modify our perceptions before the analysis function (*judgment*) begins. In addition, this pathway provides a more open-minded decision to be made because of new information that has been received. An individual can use information from the past, present, and future and decide on the relevance and reliability of this information. The challenge for the individual is how to process the information. Three steps go with this challenge: first, recognize how relevant and reliable the sources of information are; second, develop a system where one can be alerted to changing information; and third, enhance a method to frame the available sources of information. This pathway assumes that one has an adequate amount of time to go through the four steps of perception, information, judgment, and decision choice. The pathway weakens if there is a rush to make a decision because the gathering and processing of information may not be done in a proper manner.

In the decision-making process, one of these six different pathways can be used in the thought process before making a decision. *Process thinking* depicts these as having four major phases: perception, information, judgment, and decision choice. Perception frames the decision environment; it varies with each individual because it is based on an individual's personal experiences and opinions. Information is derived from all available sources and forms the basis of reliable and relevant benchmarks. Complete information is determined by its reliability and relevance to the problem to be solved. Judgment is an integration and subsequent analysis of both perception and information. In some of the pathways, the judgment phase involves compensatory and noncompensatory methods in the analysis of different situations before rendering a decision. Furthermore, many factors, both external and internal, can affect the pathways. The external factors include time pressures, incomplete information, changing environments, and expertise.

The internal factors affecting perception and judgment include strategies and biases, judgmental uncertainty, and risk-taking behavior.

Our analysis of a situation can involve compensatory and/or noncompensatory methods. Compensatory methods are conflict-confronting strategies. This method assumes that each alternative in a situation is the sum of all dimensions that can be measured on a scale and given a weight reflecting its relative importance. Two possible derivations of this method are the additive difference and the ideal point. The additive difference is the selection of an alternative based on its comparison to the other alternatives on a dimension-by-dimension basis. The ideal point is the selection of an alternative based on what an individual has as representation of what the "ideal" alternative should be. Decision choices implemented through the compensatory method result from an analysis and evaluation of the alternative having the greatest value.

Noncompensatory models are conflict-avoiding strategies that do not allow trade-offs. They are represented by four techniques: conjunctive method, disjunctive method, lexicographic method, and the elimination-by-aspects formulations. The conjunctive method requires that an individual set certain cutoff points to eliminate any alternatives that fall below these points to make a decision. The disjunctive method is used when an individual places emphasis on an alternative's best attributes, rather than on its faults, when making a decision. The lexicographic method involves making a decision by reconstructing the criteria to a narrower focus to determine the optimal decision. Finally, the elimination-by-aspects formulation is the removal of alternatives that do not provide a desired aspect, using the process of elimination to reach a decision.

The *process thinking* approach to decision making is captured in six major pathways. Each pathway has it own peculiarities, strengths, and weaknesses that can alert us to whether we are on the appropriate pathway to a decision. The four major concepts of perception, information, judgment, and decision choice can be used in varying pathway combinations. However, depending on which combination is selected, they can demonstrably influence the choices we make in life. Understanding which is the appropriate pathway to guide our reasoning may save us a great deal of time, effort, and money.

Knowledge, if recognized and used, represents power. Our knowledge pertaining to the six pathways may aid us significantly in our life endeavors. That is, these six pathways taken individually represent 1/6 or approximately 16.7 percent of accountable explanations, descriptions, or predictions about our decisions. If we rely on just one pathway exclusively for our decision-making purposes day in and day out, then it is possible that we are overlooking 83.3 percent of knowledge pertaining to decision pathways. Another way of painting this picture is that we would be allowing only one window in our house to be open to view the world. Perhaps the other windows in the house might enable us to view our world from a broader and richer perspective.

We all have been granted the opportunity to make our decisions in life. Whether on the job, at school, with family, eating at a restaurant, or socializing with friends, we are able to use our perception, acknowledge information, have our own judgment, and finally conclude with making a decision. Though we may not use all four major concepts when making a decision, we will definitely use one of the six pathways that lead to a decision. Regardless of the circumstances, our perception is typically the main aspect that drives us toward a decision. Endless scenarios may take place daily in which we will choose a unique pathway that best fits the situation that will eventually determine our process thinking.

Process thinking also provides us with the ability to know when to use the most appropriate pathway given that there is a lack of information, perceptual framing is unnecessary, no detailed analysis is required, and when all four major concepts of perception, information, judgment, and decision choice are essential for a successful decision. This particular insight can aid us to determine whether our *expertise level* is adequate to solve problems because *information* is not reliable. In addition, this insight alerts us to whether *information is reliable and relevant* for us solve problems without the benefit or use of our perceptual frames. Finally, this perspective is useful in pointing out whether our *judgment* (analysis using compensatory or noncompensatory strategies) is necessary in the situation or whether all *four major concepts* should be implemented to make a successful decision. The six pathways can be divided into four major groupings. These groupings are (1) no information, (2) lack of perceptual influences, (3) no detailed analysis (judgment), and (4) complete use of the four concepts.

No Information
P→D

P→J→D

Lack of Perceptual Influences
I→J→D

No Detailed Analysis (Judgment)
P→D

I→P→D

Complete Use of the Four Concepts
P→I→J→D

I→P→J→D

When we set out to purchase low-cost items, such as grocery shopping for dinner items, the *Expedient Pathway (P→D)* provides an efficient way of decision making given a degree of time pressures and our experience in shopping. Governance helps guide our decisions when we are involved with home, work, or social activities. The *Ruling Guide Pathway (P→J→D)* provides the necessary steps or procedures in ordering our lives. The *Analytical Pathway (I→J→D)* can assist us in understanding our return on investment of household purchases such as televisions, DVD players, washers and dryers, and so forth.

Given changing circumstances and adapting to new situations, the *Revisionist Pathway (I→P→D)* can provide us a flexible way of handling information. Career choices and relationships such as marriage, friendships, and associations rely on the *Value-Driven Pathway (P→I→J→D)* in that our personal desires and tastes typically shape and drive our selections in life. For long-term planning, such as your personal finances and education, the *Global Perspective Pathway (I→P→J→D)* can provide the best insurance for a decision-making process leading to an appropriate decision. For long-term decisions, all four major concepts provide a better picture.

In summary, *process thinking* is an ideal flexible structure that clarifies critical pathways for decision-making purposes and eliminates rival alternative tentative assumptions. It incorporates perception, information, judgment, and decision choice to reach resolution, settlement, or finding. This approach also considers external conditions such as changing environments, time pressures, incomplete information, and levels of expertise.

Being aware of perceptual influence and the use of information can influence the type of strategies we implement in our analysis. That is, the more precise the uncertainty of occurrence, information type, and the comparability of events, the higher is the likelihood of using a compensatory strategy in our judgment. Noncompensatory strategies dominate our judgment when the more *imprecise* the uncertainty of occurrence, information type, and the comparability of events.

People may implement systematically bad perceptions and judgments without knowing the appropriate pathways to successful, appropriate, and constructive decision choice. Process thinking provides a thoughtful information design that can enable us to make better decision choices.

Glossary

Analytical Pathway (I→J→D) represents a systematic and programmatic approach, which includes specifying the information (I) used in the problem, identifying all factors, weighting factors, identifying all alternatives, rating alternatives on each factor, and choosing the optimal alternative in the judgment process (J) before making a decision choice (D).

Bias is a predilection to one particular point of view or perspective. A perspective is the choice of content or a reference from which to classify, categorize, measure, or codify experience forming a representational mental state.

Confidence reflects the degree of certainty with which a decision was made. It is also represents the subjective evaluation of the reliability of the information that is being processed as well as an evaluation of the reliability of the perception and judgment process.

Decision Choice is the final concept in throughput modeling. This concept represents a culmination of perception, information, and judgment. That is, decision choice relates to how individuals use a dominant pathway to arrive at a conclusion.

Expedient Pathway (P→D) indicates a pathway from perception (P) to decision choice (D). This pathway represents an individual with a certain level of expertise or knowledge making a decision without the benefit of information because it is too noisy, incomplete, inadequately understood, or the alternatives cannot be differentiated.

Expertise relates to the enhancement and adjustment of reasoning processes in individuals' perception and judgment. That is, successful experiences reinforce already known rules or previous assumptions by experts.

Frame represents how individuals see a problem based on their stored knowledge that they use to solve a problem. Frames can be divided into general and specific ways of solving a problem. A general frame provides the context for a problem. Frames of this kind serve to give coherence and structure to the problem by placing it within a broader perspective. A specific frame defines the problem itself in terms of the available information and issues and in terms of the broader perspective of the general frame.

Global Perspective Pathway (I→P→J→D) assumes that the available information (I) influences an individual's perception (P) before a judgment (J) process is implemented to rate, rank, or order important elements of a problem before a decision choice (D) is made.

Information: data is considered as facts, and information is processed, interpreted data. Also, knowledge is personalized information.

Judgment contains the process individuals implement to analyze incoming information as well as the influences from the perception stage. From these sources, rules are implemented to weight, sort, and classify knowledge and information for problem-solving or decision-making purposes.

Knowledge: information is converted to knowledge once it is processed in the minds of individuals, and knowledge becomes information once it is articulated and presented in the form of text, graphics, words, or other symbolic forms. Hence, knowledge can be viewed as the storage and organization of information in memory.

Perception involves labeling (categorization) and arranging (classification) of information. Depending on the task at hand, individuals' perception involves their way of using knowledge to direct and guide their search of confirming or disconfirming incoming information necessary for problem solving or decision making.

Process Thinking is about different pathways we use to make a decision choice. The pathway selected by an individual can affect the type of decision made.

Revisionist Pathway (I→P→D) is highly dependent on changing information (I) resulting in a modification of how we perceive (P) a situation before making a decision choice (D).

Risk can be viewed in terms of an individual facing outcomes occurring with known or projected probability. Certainty is a special case of risk in which this probability is equal to zero or one.

Ruling Guide Pathway (P→J→D) is directed by a person's perceived (P) internal or external rules regardless of whether the present information may be contradictory. A person's perceived rules are applied in a situation and judged (J) before a decision is made (D). In this pathway, the present information available is either downplayed or ignored.

Strategies (Heuristics) are a means of saving time and effort or preprogrammed steps, resulting in simplifying strategies or rules of thumb in making decisions. They are oftentimes automatic when processing information before taking any decision action.

Throughput modeling separates process thinking into four major parts of perception (P), information (I), judgment (J), and decision choice (D). In this model perception and information are interdependent because information can influence how an individual views a problem (perception) or how he/she selects the evidence (information) to be analyzed (judgment) when making a decision choice.

Time pressures can create difficulties to examine and compare choice alternatives thereby modifying our process thinking pathway to use in making a decision choice. These changes include using heuristics, ignoring some choice alternatives altogether, making information more efficient, information selectivity, and more.

Value-Driven Pathway (P→I→J→D) indicates how an individual's perception (P) helps channel and select certain types of information (I) used in the judgment stage (J) before a decision is made.

References

Bazerman, M. H. (2005). *Judgment in managerial decision making.* New York: Wiley.

Carroll, J. S., & Johnson, E.J. (1990). *Decision Research: A Field Guide.* Newbury Park, CA: Sage Publications.

Forbes Leadership Library. (1995). *Thoughts on Success.* Chicago: Triumph Books.

Hogarth, R. M. (1987). *Judgement and choice* (2nd ed.). New York: Wiley.

Kahneman, D., Slovic, P., & Tversky, A. (1992). *Judgment under uncertainty: Heuristics and biases.* New York: Cambridge University Press.

Kahneman, D., & Tversky, A. (1973). On the psychology of prediction. *Psychological Review, 80,* 237–251.

Klein, G. (1999). *Sources of power: How people make decisions.* Boston: MIT Press.

Kleindorfer, P.R., Kunreuther, H.C., & Schoemaker, P.J.H. (1993). *Decision sciences: An integrative perspective.* New York: Cambridge University Press.

Lichtenstein, S., & Slovic, P. (1971). Reversal of preferences between bids and choices in gambling decisions. *Journal of Experimental Psychology*, 89, 46–55.

March, J. G. (1994). *A primer on decision making: How decisions happen.* New York: The Free Press.

Payne, J.W., Bettman, J.R., & Johnson, E.J. (1993). *The adaptive decision maker.* New York: Cambridge University Press.

Rodgers, W. (1984). Usefulness of decision makers' cognitive processes in a covariance structural model using financial statement information. Unpublished PhD dissertation. University of Southern California, Los Angeles.

Rodgers, W. (1991). How do loan officers make their decisions about credit risks? A study of parallel distributed processing. *Journal of Economic Psychology*, 12, 243–265.

Rodgers, W. (1992). The effects of accounting information on individuals' perceptual processes. *Journal of Accounting, Auditing, and Finance*, 7, 67–95.

Rodgers, W. (1997). *Throughput Modeling: Financial Information Used by Decision Makers.* Greenwich, CT: JAI Press.

Rodgers, W. (1999). The influences of conflicting information on novices' and loan officers' actions. *Journal of Economic Psychology*, 20, 123–145.

Rodgers, W., & Gago, S. (2006). Biblical Scriptures Underlying Six Ethical Models Influencing Organizational Practices. *Journal of Business Ethics*, 64, 125–136.

Rodgers, W., & Housel, T. (2004). The effects of environmental risk information on auditors' decisions about prospective financial statements. *European Accounting Review*, 13, 523–540.

Simon, H.A. (1957). *Models of man*. New York: Wiley.

Solso, R.L., Maclin, M.K., & Maclin, O.H. (2005). *Cognitive Psychology* (7th edition). New York: Pearson.

Tversky, A., & Kahneman, D. (1973). Availability: A heuristic for judging frequency and probability. *Cognitive Psychology*, 5, 207–232.

Tversky, A., & Kahneman, D. (1974). Judgment under uncertainty: Heuristics and biases. *Science*, 185, 1124–1131.

Tversky, A., & Kahneman, D. (1983). Extensional vs. intuitive reasoning: The conjunction fallacy in probability judgment. *Psychological Review*, 90, 293–315.

Yates, J. F. (1990). *Judgment and decision making*. Englewood Cliffs, NJ: Prentice Hall.

Index

Analytical Pathway, 3-4, 9, 15, 20-21, 23, 29, 34, 53, 79, 81, 84, 93, 109, 113, 115

Anchoring and adjustment, 43-44

Availability, 43-44, 47-50

Base rate, 46

Belief bias, 43, 69, 76, 95

Biases, 3-4, 7, 9, 11, 29, 41, 43, 53, 56, 63, 66, 69, 71, 73, 75-76, 78, 91, 94-95, 98, 100, 108-109, 111, 119, 121

Certainty, 115, 117

Compensatory, 13-14, 22, 41, 58-64, 80, 110-111, 113-114

Confidence, 37, 51, 105, 107, 115

Confirmation bias, 43-44, 69, 76, 95

Conflict avoiding, 58

Conflict confronting, 58

Conjunctive fallacy, 69, 76, 95

Decision choice, vii, 1-6, 8, 11, 14-15, 17, 19-20, 22-29, 31, 33, 35, 40-43, 52, 56-58, 60, 63, 67-68, 71, 74, 76-78, 83-84, 86, 90, 92, 98-99, 101, 106-107, 109-112, 114-118

Disjunctive model, 61

Elimination-by-aspect, 62

Expedient Pathway, 3-4, 15, 17, 20, 26, 34, 52, 65, 68-69, 71, 85-86, 108, 113, 115

Expertise, vii, 2-6, 15, 26, 33-34, 37-38, 40, 42, 59, 67, 69, 71-73, 76, 78, 88, 91, 108-110, 112, 114-116

Experts, 38-42, 74, 116

Familiarity, 48-49, 69, 76, 95

Framing, 1, 6, 11, 13, 18, 26-28, 32-33, 35-36, 40, 44, 51-53, 63-65, 73, 77-79, 85, 90-92, 100-101, 105, 108-109, 112

General frame, 37, 51, 116

Global Perspective Pathway, 3-4, 9, 15, 29-31, 34, 53, 99-100, 102, 106, 110, 114, 116

Heuristics, 117-119, 121

Hindsight, 38, 69, 76, 95

Illusory correlation, 49, 69, 76, 95

Imprecise, 7-8, 53, 55-56, 77-78, 83-84, 90, 97-98, 105-106, 109, 114

Incomplete information, vii, 2, 65-66, 108, 110, 114

Information, ii, vii-13, 15-35, 37-44, 46, 49, 51-59, 63-69, 73-74, 76-77, 79-81, 83-95, 97-102, 104-118, 120-121, 125

Judgment, vii-viii, 3, 5-6, 8, 10-11, 13, 16-23, 25-34, 38, 40-42, 51-52, 56-58, 60, 63-64, 74-75, 78, 81, 83, 86-87, 91, 94, 98, 100-101, 106-107, 109-116, 118-119, 121

Noise, 66, 69, 86, 109
Noncompensatory, 13-14, 41, 59, 61-64, 80, 110-111, 113-114

Perception, vii-viii, 2-8, 10-11, 13, 15-20, 23-31, 33-34, 38, 40-41, 44, 51-52, 56-58, 64, 66-69, 71, 74-75, 78, 81, 85-88, 91-102, 105-112, 114-118
Perceptual, 11, 13, 18, 27, 32-35, 39-40, 43-44, 53, 56, 58, 63-65, 69, 71, 77-79, 90, 92-93, 100, 102, 104-106, 108-109, 112-114, 120
Precise, 7-8, 53-55, 57, 77-78, 83-84, 89-90, 97-98, 104-106, 114
Process Thinking, vii-6, 8-12, 14-16, 18, 20-22, 24, 26-28, 30, 32-34, 36-38, 40-44, 46, 48, 50-52, 54, 56-57, 60, 62, 64, 66, 68-70, 72, 74, 76, 78, 80, 82, 84, 86, 88, 90, 94, 96, 98, 100, 102, 104, 106-108, 110-112, 114, 116-118, 120, 124

Recency, 48-49, 69, 76, 95
Representative, 43, 45-46, 50
Revisionist Pathway, 3-4, 15, 24, 26, 34, 53, 85, 88, 91, 109, 114, 117
Ruling Guide Pathway, 3-4, 9, 15, 17-18, 20, 32, 34, 52, 73, 75, 78, 100, 108, 113, 117

Satisficing, 59
Simulation, 49-50
Specific frame, 37, 51, 116

Time pressure, 26, 100

Uncertainty, 5, 7, 38, 40, 53-55, 57, 75, 100, 111, 114, 119, 121
Unstable environments, vii, 78, 90, 100, 108

Vague, 7-8, 53-57
Value-Driven Pathway, 3-4, 9, 15, 27, 29, 34, 53, 92-93, 95, 98, 109, 114, 118

About the Author

Dr. Waymond Rodgers is a CPA and a professor in the Graduate School of Management at the University of California in Riverside. He received his BA from Michigan State University, his MBA from the University of Detroit Mercy, his PhD in accounting information systems from the University of Southern California, and an experimental psychology postdoctorate from the University of Michigan. His experiences include working as an auditor with Ernst & Young and PricewaterhouseCoopers, as well as working as a commercial loan officer with Union Bank. His primary research areas are auditing, commercial lending decisions, decision modeling, ethics, trust issues, intellectual capital, and knowledge management. Professor Rodgers is widely published in accounting, ethics, information systems, management, and psychology. Finally, he is the recipient of major research grants from the Ford Foundation, National Institute of Health, National Science Foundation, Department of Defense, and the Navy Personnel Research and Development Center.

978-0-595-38950-6
0-595-38950-3

Made in the USA
Lexington, KY
12 July 2012